W9-AQK-498

52 Weekend Woodworking Projects

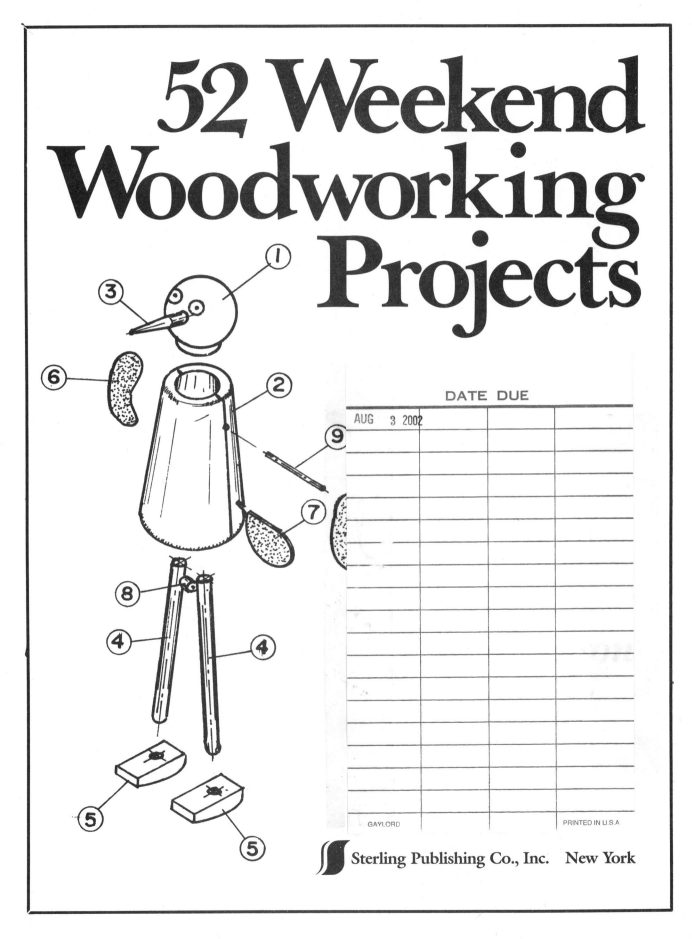

Sterling Publishing Co., Inc.   New York

Dedication

To the four "J's" in my life, my wife, Joyce, and my three daughters, Julie, Joy, and Jennifer.

Edited by R. P. Neumann

Library of Congress Cataloging-in-Publication Data

Nelson, John A., 1954–
    52 weekend woodworking projects/by John A. Nelson.
      p.   cm.
    Includes index.
    ISBN 0-8069-8300-0
    1. Woodwork.   I. Title.   II. Title: Fifty-two weekend woodworking
projects.
TT180.N46   1991
684'.08—dc20
                                       91–9954
                                         CIP

10 9 8 7 6 5 4 3

© 1991 by John A. Nelson
Published by Sterling Publishing Company, Inc.
387 Park Avenue South, New York, N.Y. 10016
Distributed in Canada by Sterling Publishing
c/o Canadian Manda Group, P.O. Box 920, Station U
Toronto, Ontario, Canada M8Z 5P9
Distributed in Great Britain and Europe by Cassell PLC
Villiers House, 41/47 Strand, London WC2N 5JE, England
Distributed in Australia by Capricorn Ltd.
P.O. Box 665, Lane Cove, NSW 2066
Manufactured in the United States of America
All rights reserved

Sterling ISBN 0-8069-8300-0

Contents

Acknowledgments

I am especially grateful to my two very good friends, Jerry Ernce, who got me started in woodworking years ago, and Bill Bigelow, who with his woodworking classes at Conval Regional High School in Peterborough, New Hampshire tested many of the designs. These two friends have also been my mentors for this book.

I extend thanks for all the effort and help from David Camp, Editor of *Popular Woodworking* magazine who, unknowingly, helped me refine my work over the years.

I want to thank Deborah Porter for taking all the photographs—I think she captured each of the projects just right.

Likewise, John Woodside, Editorial Director, Rodman Neumann, Editor, and the staff at STERLING PUBLISHING CO. have managed to transform my manuscript and art into this finished book.

I offer special appreciation and thanks to my wife Joyce for making some sense of my scribblings, my notes, and my poor English and for typing it into something sensible. She also did the painting for all the painted projects, including the sixteen horses on the carousel.

Last, but not least, I must thank my granddaughter, Hilary O'Rourke, for always pushing me to develop more toys for her.

Surely without the help of these people this book would never have been written or produced.

INTRODUCTION

All the projects in this book are designed to be made over a weekend—all fifty-two of them. A project for each weekend for a full year. I must admit, however, one or two of the projects may require a *long,* three-day weekend. Others can be put together in a weekend, but will need an extra day or two to apply a stain or paint finish. The projects range from very simple to an intermediate woodworking level—something for everyone, I hope!

The projects have been carefully chosen so that most can be made using only basic woodworking tools. A few projects do require a lathe, and one or two require the use of a band or scroll saw. If you do not have those power tools, but would like to make these projects, you might consider enrolling in an evening woodworking class for adults. Most local high schools offer these classes and have the special equipment you will need.

Because each reader will be at a different skill level and each will have completely different tools, only brief and basic instructions for making each project are given in most cases. Most projects are rather simple and, with a little thought and preparation, should be within the skill level of most woodworkers.

Each and every project has been made at least once using the finished plans and drawings so all dimensions *should* be correct by now. We have checked and rechecked each dimension and all the detail illustrations, but Murphy's law will surely prevail, so *please* recheck each dimension again before you make any cuts yourself.

Using the Drawings for Each Project

I have made every effort to clearly and fully illustrate each project—and each individual part as necessary. Each dimension has been checked and rechecked to make your work go smoothly and quickly.

With each project there is at least a two-view drawing provided. One is almost always called the *front view,* and the other is either the *side view* or the *top view.* These views are positioned in a standard way; the front view is always the most important view and the place you should start in studying the drawings. The side view is located directly to the *right* of the front view; the top view is located directly *above* the front view.

At times a *section view* is used to further illustrate a particular feature(s) of the project. The section view is sometimes a partial view that illustrates only a portion of the project such as a particular moulding detail or way of joining parts.

Most of the projects also have an *exploded view,* which fully illustrates how the project goes together. Make sure that *you* fully understand how the project is to be assembled *before* any work is started.

The drawings throughout this book *number* each and every part. Each part is called-off in as many views as possible so that you can see *exactly* where each part is located. A box accompanies each set of drawings that serves as a *bill of materials* list. Each part is listed, *in order,* using the same number *and* noting its name, its overall size, and exactly *how many* of each part is required.

Multiple parts should be made exactly the same size and shape. Every now and then a project requires a *pair* of parts, that is, a right-hand piece and a left-hand piece. In such a case, take care not to make duplicate pieces, but rather a left-hand and right-hand pair. In most projects requiring a pair, this is noted—but for any "multiple" parts double-check if in doubt.

Throughout, as practical, I numbered all the parts in the order that I would *suggest* you make and assemble them. You might want to make and assemble your project some other way, but this is what worked best for me and is how I made them.

For some of the projects, I have pictured in the drawings the actual parts I used, as shown in the photographs. Depending on the particular parts you are able to obtain, you may need to make slight alterations in the plans to accommodate any size variation. Many times the same or essentially equivalent part or parts can be purchased from several companies. It is a good idea to obtain as many suppliers' catalogs as possible and look for the best products at the best prices.

Making the Project

After you thoroughly study the project, start by carefully making each individual part. Take care to make each piece exactly to the correct size and exactly *square*—that is, each cut at 90 degrees to the face—as required.

Sand each individual piece, but take care to keep all the edges sharp—**do not round the edges** at this time—some will be rounded *after* assembly.

After all the pieces have been made with great care, "dry-fit" the pieces—that is, cautiously put together the entire project to check for correct fit throughout before final assembly. If anything needs refitting, this is the time to correct it.

When the pieces all fit correctly, glue and/or nail the project together, again taking care that all fits are tight and square. Sand the project all over; it is at this time that edges can be "rounded," if necessary. The project is then ready for finishing.

Today, the trend is towards using the metric system of measure; therefore, a Metric Conversion Chart, is provided for quick conversion on page 160.

Enlarging a Pattern or Design

Many of the drawings are reduced relative to the actual size of the parts so that all of the information can be presented on the page. In some projects, the patterns for various irregular parts or irregular portions of parts must be enlarged to full size. A grid of squares are drawn over these parts and the original size of the grid is noted on the drawing.

There are four ways a design or shape of the irregular part or parts can be enlarged to full size.

Method One

One of the simplest and most inexpensive ways is to use an ordinary office-type photocopy machine. Most of these newer machines have an enlarging/reducing feature. Simply put the book page on the machine, choose the enlargement mode you need (usually expressed as a percentage of the original) and make a copy. In extreme cases, you may have to make *another* copy of the enlargement copy in order to get the required size—sometimes you must make more than two copies. In some cases you will not be able to get the exact required size but the result will be close enough for most work, perhaps requiring a little touching-up, at most.

Method Two

A very quick and extremely accurate method is to go to a local commercial "Quick-Printer" and ask them to make a P.M.T. (photomechanical transfer) of the area needed to be enlarged or reduced. This is a photographic method that yields an *exact* size without any difficulty. This method will cost about five to fifteen dollars, depending on the size of the final P.M.T.—if your time is valuable, it might be worth the cost.

Method Three

Another simple, quick method is to use a drawing tool called the *pantograph*. It is an inexpensive tool that is very simple to use for enlarging or reducing to most any required size. If you do a lot of enlarging or reducing, the cost of this tool may be well worth the price.

Method Four

Most authors assume woodworkers will use the grid and dot-to-dot method. It is very simple; you do not have to be an artist to use the method. This method can be used to enlarge or reduce to *any size* or scale. This method requires eight simple steps:

Step 1: Note what size the full-size grid should be—this is usually indicated on the drawing near the grid. Most of the grids used with the project drawings must be redrawn so that each square is one-half inch or one inch per side.

Step 2: Calculate the overall required width and height. If it is *not* given, simply count the squares across and down and multiply by the size of each square. For example, a one-half inch grid with 15 squares across requires an overall width of 7½ inches. The paper size needed to draw the pattern full size should be a little larger than the overall size of the part.

Step 3: Note: it would be helpful if you have a few basic drafting tools but not necessary. Tools suggested are: a drafting board, a scale (ruler), a T-square, a 45 degree triangle, masking tape, and a sheet of paper a little larger than the required overall size of the pattern. Tape the paper to the drafting board or other surface and carefully draw the required grid on the paper using the drafting tools or whatever tools you have.

Step 4: On the original reduced drawing in the book, start from the upper left corner and add *letters* across the top of the grid from left to right, A through whatever letter it takes to get to the other side of the grid. From the same starting point, add *numbers* down, from 1 to whatever number it takes to get to the bottom of the grid.

Step 5: On your full-size grid, add letters and numbers in exactly the same way as the original.

Step 6: On the original reduced drawing, draw dots along the pattern outline wherever it crosses the grid.

Step 7: On your full-size grid, locate and draw the same dots on the grid. It is helpful to locate each dot by using the letters across the top and the numbers along the side. For example, a dot at B-6 can easily be found on the new, full-size grid by coming down from line B and over on line 6.

Step 8: All that is left to do is to connect the dots. Note: you do not have to be exact, all you have to do is to sketch a line between the dots using your eye to approximate the shape of the original reduced drawing.

Transferring the Pattern From Paper to Wood

Tape the full-size pattern to the wood with carbon paper in between for transferring the pattern. If you are going to copy the pattern many times, make a template instead. Simply transfer the pattern onto a sheet of heavy cardboard or 1/8-inch thick hardboard or plywood and cut out the pattern. This template can then be used over an over by simply tracing around the template to lay out the pattern for each copy.

If the pattern is symmetrical—that is, the exact same size and shape on both sides of an imaginary line, make only a *half-pattern* and trace it twice, once on each side of the midline. This will ensure the perfect symmetry of the finished part.

For small patterns—8 1/2 inches by 11 inches or smaller at full size—make a photocopy of the full-size pattern using any copy machine. Tape the copy, printed side down, and, using a hot flat iron or hot wood-burning set, heat the back side of the copy. The pattern will transfer from the paper directly to the wood. This method is very good for very small or complicated patterns.

Selecting Material for Your Project

As lumber will probably be the most expensive material you will purchase for each project, it is a good idea that you have some basic knowledge about lumber so that you can make wise choices and save a little money here and there on your purchases.

All lumber is divided into two kinds, hardwood and softwood. Hardwoods are deciduous trees, trees that flower and lose their leaves seasonally; softwoods are the coniferous trees, which are cone-bearing and mostly evergreen. In actuality, a few "hardwoods" are softer than some "softwoods"—but on the whole, hardwoods are harder, closer grained, much more durable, tougher to work, and take a stain beautifully. Hardwood typically costs more than softwood, but it is well worth it.

All wood contains pores—open spaces that served as water-conducting vessels—which are more noticeable in some kinds than in others. Woods such as oak and mahogany have pores that are very noticeable and probably should be filled for the best finished appearance. Woods such as maple and birch have what is called close-grain, which provides a beautiful smooth finish.

The *grain* of wood is the result of each year's growth of new cells. Around the tree's circumference each year annular growth forms a new and hard fibrous layer. Growth in most trees is seasonal but somewhat regular so that these rings are evenly spaced. In other trees this annular growth is not very regular, thus creating uneven spacing and thickness. The patterns formed by the rings when the tree is cut into lumber is what we see as the grain pattern.

The softwoods I used for most of the projects are pine, spruce, and fir. Pine is a good choice since it is the easiest to work, especially for the simpler projects.

Of the hardwoods I most used maple, walnut, oak, cherry, poplar, and birch. For most projects I note what wood was used in making the completed piece shown in the photograph that accompanies the instructions.

Always buy "dried" lumber, as green lumber may shrink, twist or warp while drying. Purchase the best lumber you can find for these projects since each of them does not take much material at all. Your work will be much easier and your finished project will be much better for the better quality wood. The actual cost difference between an inexpensive piece of wood and the best you can find will be quite small since the overall cost of any of these projects is very low to begin with. As a general rule I recommend that you purchase the very best wood you can get at all times.

Lumber is sold by the *board foot*. A board foot is a piece of wood that is one-foot wide, one-inch thick, and one-foot long. A piece of wood four-inches wide (one-third of a foot) one-inch thick, and twelve-feet long contains four board feet of wood. The formula is: width in feet times thickness in inches times length in feet. (One-third times one times twelve = four board feet.)

Finding Board Feet Using a Factor

Using the table below to find the appropriate factor, we can easily calculate that a board one-inch thick, five-inches wide, and 12-feet long can be converted to board feet by multiplying 12 (linear length) times 0.417 (factor) to give 5.004 board feet of lumber. (The term linear length refers to the actual length of any board as it is measured.)

BOARD FEET USING LINEAR LENGTH			
1/2" THICK BOARD		1" THICK BOARD	
WIDTH	FACTOR	WIDTH	FACTOR
2	.083	2	.167
3	.125	3	.250
4	.166	4	.333
5	.209	5	.417
6	.250	6	.500
8	.333	8	.666
10	.417	10	.833
12	.500	12	1.000

TO FIND BOARD FEET MULTIPLY THE LENGTH
OF THE BOARD TIMES THE ABOVE FACTOR

Dressed lumber comes in actual sizes other than the nominal size would indicate because of the finishing process. For example, a one-by-six measures about 3/4 inch by 5 5/8 inches in actual size. The chart below indicates what some of the actual sizes may be. Note: today, the actual width may vary—in some areas a one-by-six might be 5 1/2-inches wide rather than 5 5/8-inches wide. Check around in your area before buying wood.

ROUGH SIZE	FINISHED SIZE
1 X 2	3/4 X 1 5/8
1 X 3	3/4 X 2 5/8
1 X 4	3/4 X 3 5/8
1 X 5	3/4 X 4 5/8
1 X 6	3/4 X 5 5/8
1 X 8	3/4 X 7 5/8
1 X 10	3/4 X 9 1/2
1 X 12	3/4 X 11 1/2

A few projects call for wide boards. I believe the project would look best if you could find the required width. If this is not possible, glue narrower boards together by edge-joining them to produce the necessary width. Try to match grain patterns with great care so that each joint will not be so noticeable. Even though I prefer the look of the single wide board, I should point out that a glued joint is stronger than a single piece of wood and probably will not warp.

Hardware for Your Project

The extra money spent on hardware of high quality versus that saved on low-cost hardware is—as noted in purchasing lumber—a very small difference since the overall cost of your project is already quite low. Don't forget, the hardware is usually what is most visible, so the little extra spent will be well worth the increased look of quality for many years to come.

Kinds of Joint

Most of the projects in this text use only basic kinds of joint: The *butt joint*, the *rabbet joint*, and the *dado joint*. These can easily be made by hand, without power tools—if you do have the power tools, use them since it will make the job even easier.

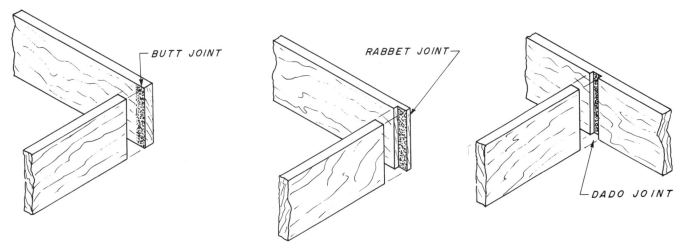

Most of the simpler projects use the butt joint. This is the simplest of all joints and, as its name implies, is simply two boards that are butted up against each other and joined together, perhaps with glue and nails or screws. The major disadvantage of the butt joint is that there is less surface area available for gluing or nailing than for other joints. Nails sometimes back out of the joint over time, which also makes an opening at the joint. A rabbet joint is an L-shaped cutout made along the edge or end of one board to overlap the edge or end of the mating board. This joint can also be nailed and/or glued together. Because rabbet joints are often cut into side pieces, the nails—put in from the sides—may be hidden somewhat from view. Dado joints are similar to rabbet joints except the cut is made leaving wood shoulders on both sides. A drawer side is an excellent example of the use of both a dado joint and a rabbet joint.

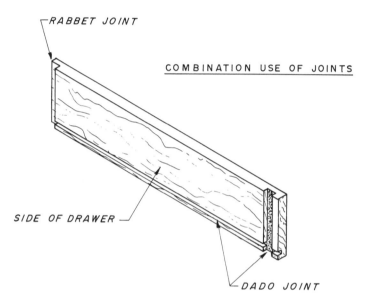

RABBET JOINT

COMBINATION USE OF JOINTS

SIDE OF DRAWER

DADO JOINT

Gluing

Wood glues are called either "hot" or "cold," depending on whether or not heat is used to prepare them. The "hot" glue is made from animal parts, which make the glue—commonly called hide glue—very strong and quick-setting. Hide glue used to be only available as flakes which required heating. Now hide glue is available in liquid form for application without heating. Until very recently old-fashioned hide glue was considered the *only* true, satisfactory kind of glue to use in cabinetmaking. Recent developments in new and better cold glues have made this generalization debatable. Cold glues are all derived from synthetic material of one kind or another. They vary in durability and strength. For the simpler projects cold glue is, by far, the easiest to use, and I recommend its use. In using cold glue, always follow the instructions given on the label.

When gluing, always take care to clean all excess glue from around the joint. This is a *must* if you are going to stain the project. The excess glue will not take the stain and will appear white. I find that by waiting for 10 to 15 minutes, just until the glue is almost set, I can carefully remove most of it with a sharp wood chisel. Do not wipe off the excess glue with a wet cloth as the water will weaken the glue joint and possibly spread glue into the pore space irretrievably, staining the wood.

Glue was not in general use until after 1750. Therefore, some of the original pieces on which many of the "Country" projects were based may simply have been nailed together—or possibly some may have used locking joints such as a sliding dovetail or mortise-and-tenon with wood pegs. If, by chance, they actually were glued together, they were probably joined with "hot" animal—or hide—glue.

Finishing

Once you have completed assembling your project, you are then ready to apply a finish. This is the important part and should not be rushed. If it takes eight hours to make the project, plan on eight hours to finish it correctly.

Preparing

Step 1: All joints should be checked for tight fits. If necessary apply water putty to all joints—allow ample time for drying.

Step 2: Sand the project all over in the direction of the wood grain. If sanding is done by hand, use a sanding block, and be careful to keep all corners still *sharp*. Sand all over using an 80 grit sandpaper. Resand all over using a 120 grit sandpaper, and, if necessary, sand again all over using a 180 grit sandpaper. Take care not to "round" edges at this time.

Step 3: If you do want any of the edges rounded, use the 120 grit sandpaper, and later the 180 grit sandpaper, specifically to round the edges.

Step 4: I personally think the "country" projects should look old. A copy of an antique that looks new seems somehow to be a direct contradiction. Distressing—making the piece look old—can be done in many ways. Using a piece of coral stone about three inches in diameter, or a similar object, roll the stone across the various surfaces. Don't be afraid to add a few random scratches here and there, especially on the bottom or back where an object would have been worn the most. Using a rasp, judiciously round the edges where you think wear would have occurred. Resand the entire project and the new "worn" edges with 180 grit sandpaper.

Step 5: Clean all surfaces with a damp rag to remove all dust.

A paste filler should be used for porous wood such as oak, ash, or mahogany. Purchase paste filler that is slightly darker than the color of your wood as the new wood you used will turn darker with age. Before using paste filler, thin it with turpentine so it can be applied with a brush. Use a stiff brush, and brush with the grain in order to fill the pores. Wipe off with a piece of burlap across the grain, after 15 or 20 minutes, taking care to leave filler in the pores. Apply a second coat if necessary; let it dry for 24 hours.

Staining

There are two major kinds of stain; water-base stain and oil-base stain. Water stain has a tendency to raise the grain of the wood, so that after it dries, the surface should be lightly sanded with fine sandpaper. Oil stain does not raise the grain.

Step 1: Test the stain color on a scrap piece of the same kind of lumber to make certain it will be the color you wish.

Step 2: Wipe or brush on the stain as quickly and as evenly as possible to avoid overlapping streaks. If a darker finish is desired, apply more than one coat of stain. Try not to apply too much stain on the end grain. Allow to dry in a dust-free area for at least 24 hours.

Finishes

Shellac is a hard, easy-to-apply finish and dries in a few hours. For best results, thin slightly with alcohol and apply an extra coat or two. Several coats of thin shellac are much better than one or two thick coats. Sand lightly with extra-fine sandpaper between coats, but be sure to rub the entire surface with a dampened cloth. For the "country" projects, strive for a smooth, satin finish—not a high-gloss finish coat. It will give your project that "antique" look.

Varnish is easy to brush on and dries to a smooth, hard finish within 24 hours. It makes an excellent finish that is transparent and will give a deep finish look to your project. Be sure to apply varnish in a completely dust-free area. Apply one or two coats directly from the can with long, even strokes. Rub between each coat, and after the last coat, with 0000 steel wool.

Oil finishes are especially easy to use for projects such as those in this book. Oil finish is easy to apply, long lasting, never needs resanding, and actually improves wood permanently. Apply a heavy, wet coat uniformly to all surfaces, and allow to set for 20 or 30 minutes. Wipe completely dry until you have a pleasing finish.

Wash Coat

The wash coat is an option for obtaining that real old "country" look. Notice that your "country" project probably still looks "new"—even with the distressing marks and scratches. To give your project a one-hundred-year-old look, simply wipe a coat of oil-base black paint directly from the can with a cloth. Take care to get the black paint in all the distressed marks and scratches. Wipe all of the paint off immediately before it dries, but leave the black paint in all the corners, joints, scratches, and distress marks. This takes a little experience, but, if you goof, simply wipe it off using a cloth with turpentine on it. This coat should make your project look like a very old antique.

Painted Projects

Use a high-quality paint, either oil or water base. Today, the trend is towards water-base paint. Prime your project, and lightly sand after it dries. Apply two *light* coats of paint rather than one thick coat. I like to add water to thin water-base paint slightly since I feel that water-base paint tends to be a little thick. For all toy projects, be sure to use a nontoxic paint at all times.

For a very satisfying "feel" to the finish, I usually apply an overall coat of paste wax as the final step.

THE 52 WEEKEND PROJECTS

HOUSEHOLD PROJECTS

1 ◆ Cutting Board

Cutting boards come in all shapes and sizes. I have seen pigs, chickens, turkeys, and even rabbits as cutting boards. This design is a simple rectangle with a round handle. Most any kind of hardwood and most any thickness of wood can be used. One-inch thick ash was used for the one pictured.

Instructions

Carefully lay out the full-size pattern on a piece of cardboard about 12 inches by 22 inches in size. Cut out the full-size pattern, and transfer the shape to the wood. If you have to glue up material to get the full 11-inch wide board, be sure to use waterproof glue.

Carefully cut out the cutting board, and sand all edges and surfaces. Using a three-eighths-inch radius router bit with a ball-bearing follower, rout the top and bottom edges, and then resand all over.

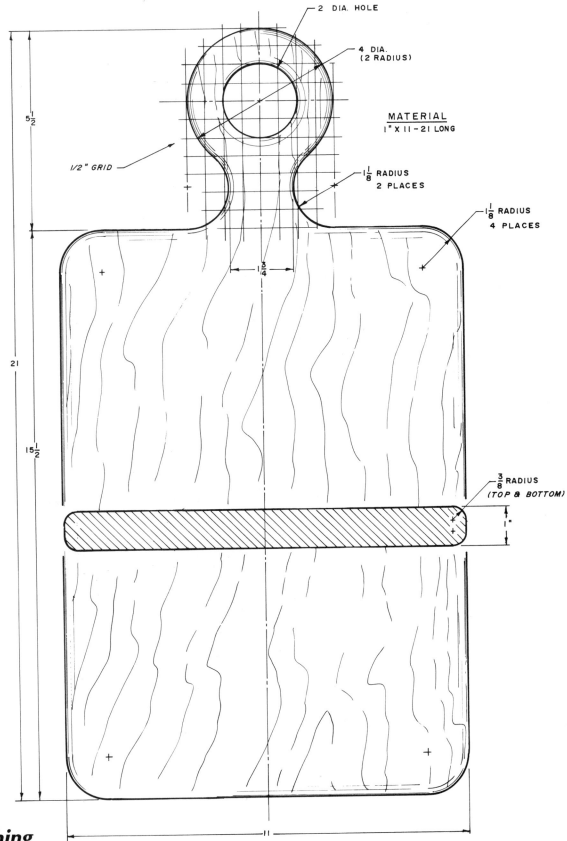

Finishing

Be sure to use a finish that is nontoxic, such as one labelled "salad bowl" finish. As cutting boards are very popular, keep your full-size pattern. You probably will be making more than one cutting board, especially after everyone sees the first one.

2 ♦ Clipboard

You can buy clipboards made of cheap pressboard, but any self-respecting woodworker needs a clipboard made of real *wood*, perhaps even exotic wood. I made this one out of scrap pieces of mahogany that I had around and just hated to burn up.

Instructions

Glue up material to make up the 9-inch by 13-inch board, if necessary. Use pieces of wood with pleasing grain patterns. Plane the wood to 1/4-inch or 5/16-inch thick. (It is okay to leave the wood a little thick.) Sand all over.

Cut to exact size, and round the four corners. Locate and drill the two 3/16-inch diameter holes for the screws to hold the clip in place. Locate and drill from the *bottom* surface for the screws to hold the four feet in place. Take care *not* to drill through.

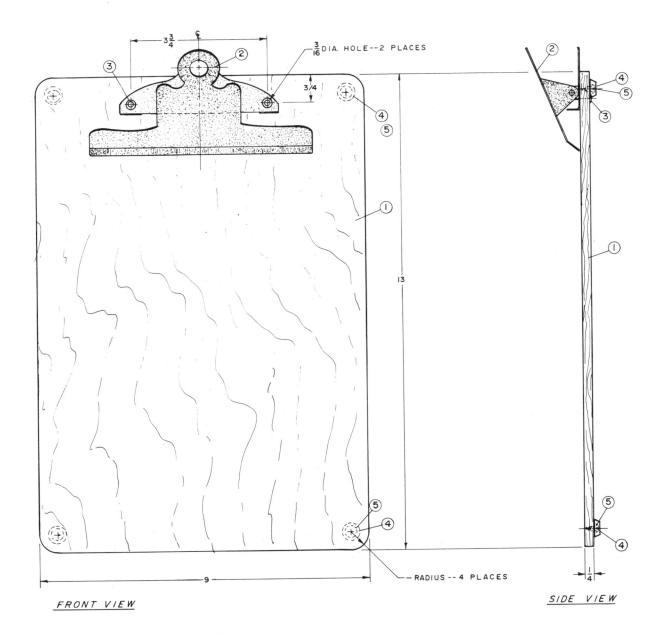

$3\frac{3}{4}$

$\frac{3}{16}$ DIA. HOLE -- 2 PLACES

3/4

13

9

RADIUS -- 4 PLACES

1/4

FRONT VIEW

SIDE VIEW

NO.	NAME	SIZE	REQ'D.
1	BOARD	1/4 (3/8) X 9 - 13 LONG	1
2	CLIP	6" SIZE	1
3	SCREW POST		2
4	FOOT W/NO. 10 SC..	421/20	4
5	SCREW FOR FOOT		4

Sand all over with a fine grit sandpaper. Do not round the edges. Apply two or three coats of a clear, hard finish on top, bottom, and edges. Lightly sand between coats.

Assemble the clip and four feet. Now this is a *woodworker's* clipboard!

3 ◆ Simple Tool Box

Here is a simple tool box that can be used for all kinds of things, *even* tools! If necessary, to fit a particular need, you can make it longer than 14 inches.

The tool box can be made of any kind of wood, but a hardwood is recommended.

Instructions

Cut parts to size per the cutting list. Take care to make all cuts at 90 degrees. Sand all surfaces with medium grit sandpaper. Cut the two ends to shape according to the plans. It is a good idea to *tape* two pieces of stock together to cut both ends at the same time. This way both will be *exactly* the same size and shape.

If a hard wood is used, it is a good idea to predrill for all the nails, so that the wood does not split.

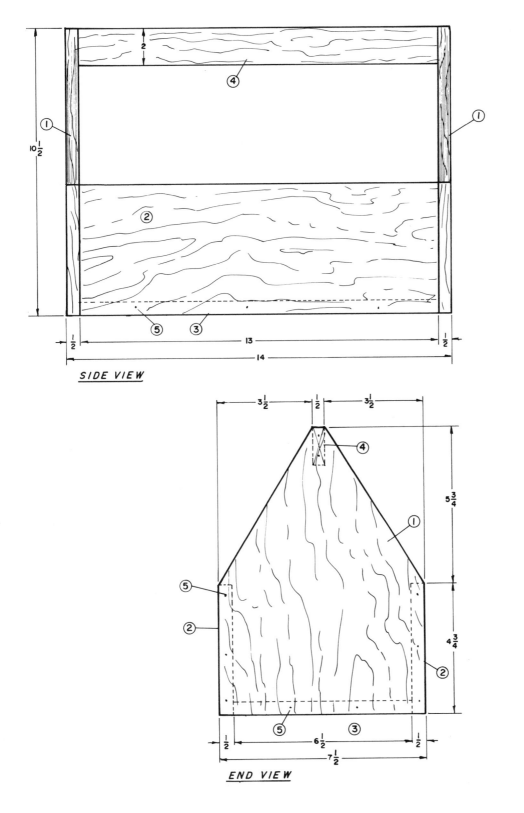

SIDE VIEW

END VIEW

NO.	NAME	SIZE	REQ'D.
1	END	1/2 X 7 1/2 -10 1/2 LG.	2
2	SIDE	1/2 X 4 3/4 -13 LG.	2
3	BOTTOM	1/2 X 6 1/2 -13 LONG	1
4	HANDLE	1/2 X 2 -13 LONG	1
5	FINISH NAIL	6 d	28

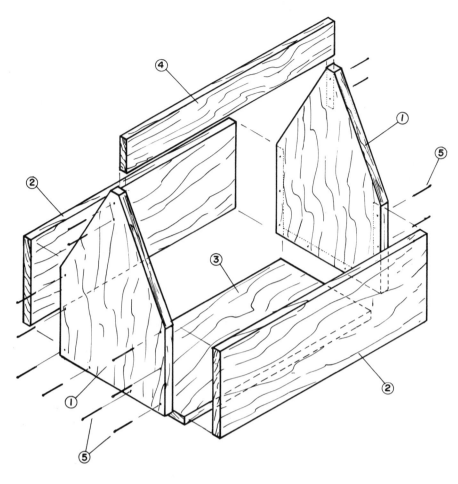

EXPLODED VIEW

All joints are simple butt joints making this tool box easy to put together. Glue and nail all joints, taking care to keep everything square as you assemble the box. Add the handle last. After assembly, resand all over, but keep all the edges sharp.

This project can be finished with either a stain and clear top coat or painted. Now you can get *all* your tools in one place ready for any emergency.

4 ◆ Four-Drawer Bookcase Unit

You *never* have enough storage areas, especially if you are a "collector" like I am. Here are drawer units that can be used *vertically* or *horizontally,* or both. They do not take up much space and can fit most anywhere. Don't let the four drawers intimidate you. A drawer is nothing more than a box with the top missing. The drawer construction for this project is a little different than most drawer construction: it is a simplified drawer, easy to make.

Instructions

Cut all pieces per the parts list, keeping all cuts at 90 degrees. Carefully locate and make the three 1/2-inch wide, 1/4-inch deep dado cuts and the two 1/2-inch wide, 1/4-inch deep rabbets in the two sides. Take care as these cuts must be accurate. You must maintain the four-inch dimension between each drawer divider. Cut the 1/4-inch wide, 1/4-inch deep rabbet along the inner *back* edge of the sides as shown. Take care to make a left- and right-hand *pair* of sides.

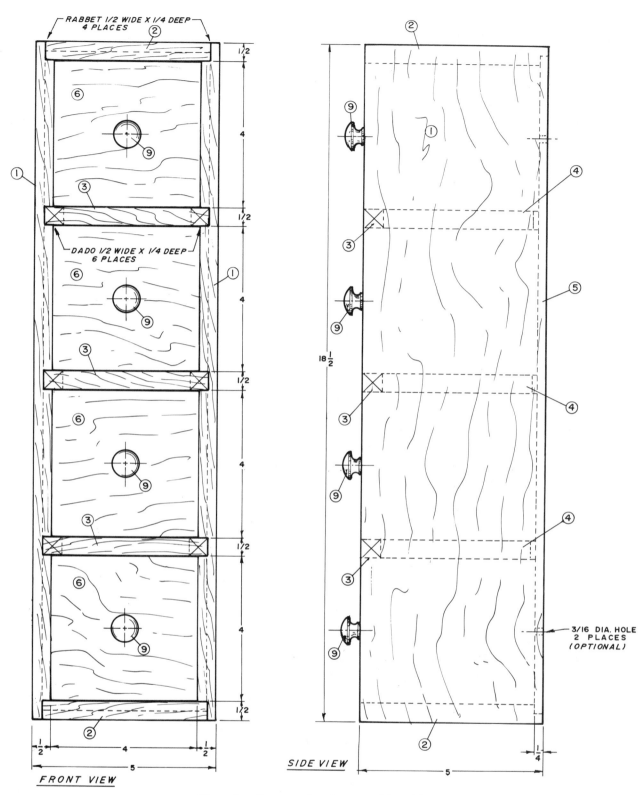

RABBET 1/2 WIDE X 1/4 DEEP
4 PLACES

DADO 1/2 WIDE X 1/4 DEEP
6 PLACES

FRONT VIEW

SIDE VIEW

3/16 DIA. HOLE
2 PLACES
(OPTIONAL)

Glue the drawer dividers and backboard in place taking care that every-thing is square. Add the drawer supports. Apply glue to only the front half of each support to allow for expansion. This is a good tip whenever you are gluing wood together and the grain of one piece is running at 90 degrees to the grain of the other. Check that each drawer opening is exactly four inches *square*.

Cut the pieces for the drawers using a "saw stop" on your saw. Each matching piece *must* be exactly the same size and shape; the saw stop will

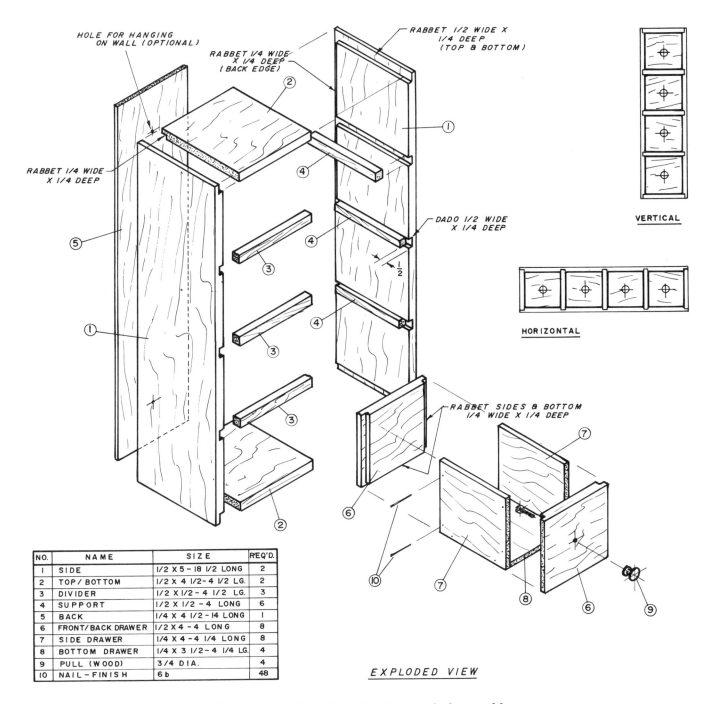

HOLE FOR HANGING
ON WALL (OPTIONAL)

RABBET 1/4 WIDE
X 1/4 DEEP
(BACK EDGE)

RABBET 1/2 WIDE X
1/4 DEEP
(TOP & BOTTOM)

RABBET 1/4 WIDE
X 1/4 DEEP

DADO 1/2 WIDE
X 1/4 DEEP

RABBET SIDES & BOTTOM
1/4 WIDE X 1/4 DEEP

VERTICAL

HORIZONTAL

EXPLODED VIEW

NO.	NAME	SIZE	REQ'D.
1	SIDE	1/2 X 5 – 18 1/2 LONG	2
2	TOP/BOTTOM	1/2 X 4 1/2 – 4 1/2 LG.	2
3	DIVIDER	1/2 X 1/2 – 4 1/2 LG.	3
4	SUPPORT	1/2 X 1/2 – 4 LONG	6
5	BACK	1/4 X 4 1/2 – 14 LONG	1
6	FRONT/BACK DRAWER	1/2 X 4 – 4 LONG	8
7	SIDE DRAWER	1/4 X 4 – 4 1/4 LONG	8
8	BOTTOM DRAWER	1/4 X 3 1/2 – 4 1/4 LG.	4
9	PULL (WOOD)	3/4 DIA.	4
10	NAIL – FINISH	6 b	48

ensure that they are. Carefully cut the 1/4-inch wide, 1/4-inch deep rabbets on both the inner side and *bottom* edge of each drawer front; see the exploded view.

Dry-fit all of the drawer parts, and check that the drawer fronts are just a little *under* four inches square. Fit one drawer into the opening to make sure that it fits correctly. Make adjustments on the parts, if necessary. Glue and nail the drawer units together. Carefully find the middle of the drawer fronts (draw two lines diagonally from corner to corner to find the exact middle). Drill a hole in each front for the screw to secure the 3/4-inch diameter knobs.

After everything is assembled, sand the case and each drawer with medium and then fine grit sandpaper. Clean off all dust with a tack rag.

Prime and paint all outer surfaces. Now you have a place for all those important things you just can't bear to throw away.

25

5 ♦ Sewing Box with Three Drawers

Here is a project for anyone who sews a lot or knows someone who does. It is a takeoff of an original antique sewing box. It is an interesting design as there are no drawer dividers. All you can see are the three drawer fronts. I made the one pictured out of red oak, but any wood could be used.

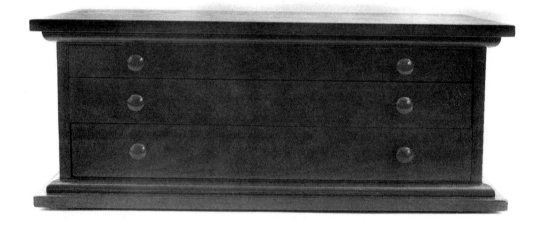

Instructions

Cut all the parts to size, and sand all surfaces with fine grit paper. Make the two notches on the inner surfaces of the end pieces, 1/2-inch wide, 1/4-inch deep. Also cut the 1/4-inch wide, 1/4-inch deep rabbet in the back edge. Be sure to make a left- and right-hand *pair* of ends.

For *this* project I would suggest you work backwards, that is, make the drawers *first* and then fit the drawer supports and case around the drawers. Cut the required dadoes and rabbets for the drawers, and assemble the drawers in the manner shown in the exploded view. Be sure *all* the drawers are exactly *square* and that all three are exactly the same overall size; 9 3/16 inches wide and 18 inches long.

I am sure there are many ways to construct the drawer supports and case, but here is how I did it. Add two layers of masking tape to the top and bottom surfaces of each assembled drawer. Now tape all three drawers together to form one large drawer unit. To get exact and correct drawer support locations, place the drawer supports *into* the drawer dadoes. With the drawer supports in the drawer dadoes, apply a little glue to the drawer supports.

With care, temporarily tape the case *side* to the three drawers in the position it will be when the case is assembled. Carefully push each drawer support one-quarter inch *in* from the front edge as shown in the right end subassembly. This will give you the exact location on each side for the three drawer supports.

After the glue sets, untape the sides from the drawers. Once you are sure all the drawer supports are positioned correctly, nail them in place using 1/2-inch long brads. (This will allow for any expansion.)

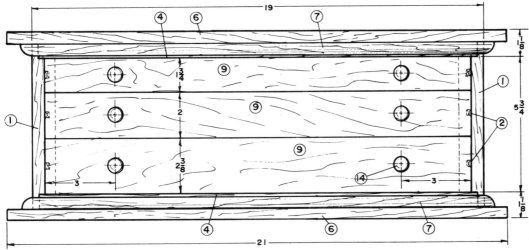

FRONT VIEW

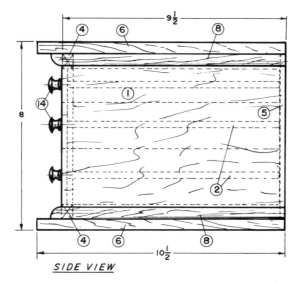

SIDE VIEW

NO.	NAME	SIZE	REQ'D.
1	END	1/2 X 7 - 9 1/2 LG.	2
2	DRAWER SUPPORT	3/16 X 1/4 - 9 LONG	6
3	BRAD	1/2 LONG	18
4	RAIL	1/2 X 5/8 - 18 1/2 LG.	2
5	BACK	1/4 X 7 - 18 1/2 LG.	1
6	TOP / BOTTOM	1/2 X 10 1/2 - 21 LG.	2
7	MOLDING	1/2 ROUND - 20 LG.	2
8	MOLDING - END	1/2 ROUND - 10 LONG	4
9	DRAWER FRONT	1/2 X 1 3/8 - 18 LG.	1
		1/2 X 2 - 18 LONG	1
		1/2 X 2 3/8 - 18 LG.	1
10	DRAWER BACK	1/2 X 1 3/8 - 17 1/2 LG.	1
		1/2 X 2 - 17 1/2 LONG	1
		1/2 X 2 3/8 - 17 1/2 LG.	1
11	DRAWER SIDE	1/2 X 1 3/8 - 8 15/16	2
		1/2 X 2 - 8 15/16 LG.	2
		1/2 X 2 3/8 - 8 15/16	2
12	DRAWER BOTTOM	1/8 X 8 9/16 - 17 3/8	3
13	NAIL - FINISH	1" LONG	AS REQ'D
14	DRAWER PULL	5/8 DIA.	6

27

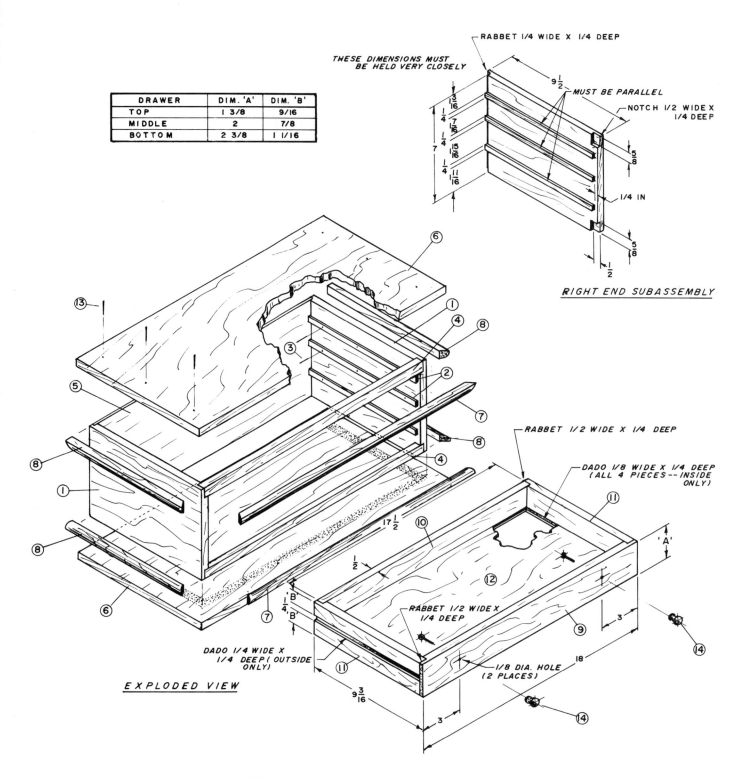

DRAWER	DIM. 'A'	DIM. 'B'
TOP	1 3/8	9/16
MIDDLE	2	7/8
BOTTOM	2 3/8	1 1/16

THESE DIMENSIONS MUST
BE HELD VERY CLOSELY

RABBET 1/4 WIDE X 1/4 DEEP

MUST BE PARALLEL

NOTCH 1/2 WIDE X 1/4 DEEP

1/4 IN

RIGHT END SUBASSEMBLY

RABBET 1/2 WIDE X 1/4 DEEP

DADO 1/8 WIDE X 1/4 DEEP
(ALL 4 PIECES -- INSIDE ONLY)

RABBET 1/2 WIDE X 1/4 DEEP

1/8 DIA. HOLE
(2 PLACES)

DADO 1/4 WIDE X
1/4 DEEP (OUTSIDE
ONLY)

EXPLODED VIEW

Add two layers of masking tape along the sides of the drawers, and build the case around the taped drawers. The two layers of tape will give you a good clearance around each drawer. Adjust the fit of the case pieces, if necessary, so that the case fits snugly around the taped drawers. Glue and nail the assembly together. After the glue sets, remove the drawers and untape everything. Refit the drawers; they should fit nicely with a slight space around each.

Locate the holes for drawer pulls three inches in from each end. Stain or paint your sewing box. It will be enjoyed for years to come, and not just for keeping sewing supplies.

6 ♦ Folding Side Table

A while back I made a set of Adirondack lawn chairs. They were great and we enjoyed them, but occasionally we wanted to eat outdoors sitting in the Adirondack chairs, so I developed this folding side table. The year before, I had designed a folding stool, so I simply redesigned the folding stool to make up this folding side table. During the winter months, it folds up so that it is easily stored.

Instructions

Cut all the pieces to exact size. Use a saw stop or a jig to ensure that matching parts are exactly the same size.

Carefully cut the ends of the legs and support part nos. 1 and 2. Locate and drill the 1/2-inch diameter holes. Again, use drilling jigs, if possible, to ensure that all the parts match the given dimensions. Sand all the parts on all edges and surfaces.

Study the exploded view drawings. It is extremely important that the parts are assembled exactly as shown. The table can be either nailed or screwed together. Note edge surface "A" on each support and "B" on each leg in the detailed drawings.

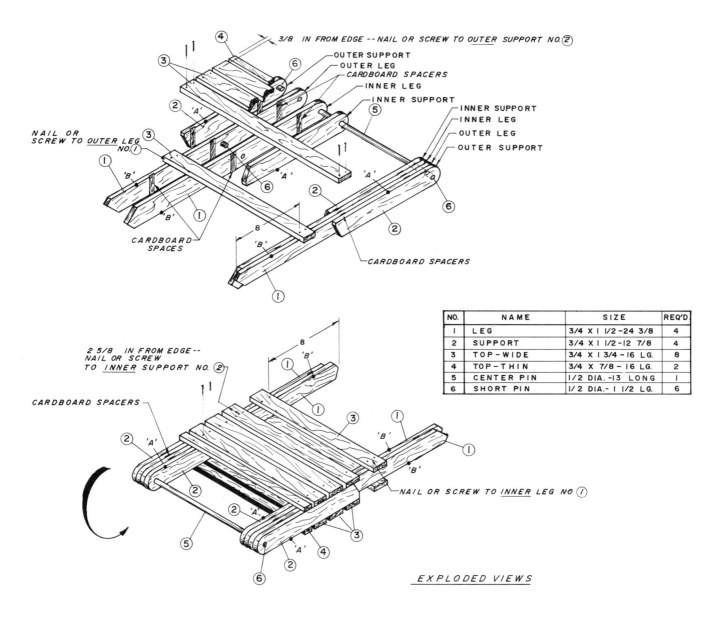

NO.	NAME	SIZE	REQ'D
1	LEG	3/4 X 1 1/2 -24 3/8	4
2	SUPPORT	3/4 X 1 1/2 -12 7/8	4
3	TOP-WIDE	3/4 X 1 3/4 - 16 LG.	8
4	TOP-THIN	3/4 X 7/8 - 16 LG.	2
5	CENTER PIN	1/2 DIA. -13 LONG	1
6	SHORT PIN	1/2 DIA.- 1 1/2 LG.	6

EXPLODED VIEWS

Refer to the upper drawing of the exploded views: Add the two inner supports, part no. 2, to the center pin, part no. 5, and add two inner legs, part no. 1, exactly as shown. Check the drawing to make sure the corresponding edge surfaces, 'A' and 'B,' are oriented correctly. Attach one short pin, part no. 6, to the middle hole of each of the two legs. Attach the two outer legs, part no. 1, to the assembly at the middle hole. Be sure that edge surfaces correspond exactly with the drawing.

Add the two remaining short pins, part no. 6, to the top hole of the outer legs and add the outer supports, part no. 2. Be sure edge surface "B" is *up*. Cut about 14 cardboard spacers, one inch by two inches, and insert them between the legs and supports as shown. Check that everything is square. Nail three wide tops, part no. 3, and one thin top, part no. 4, to the *outer* support keeping a 7/16-inch space between the top boards. Attach an extra top board, part no. 3, to the outer legs, eight inches *up* from the bottom. Check that everything is square and that the legs are still parallel to each other.

Refer to the lower drawing of the exploded views: Carefully turn the assembly over with the spacers intact, and nail the wide and thin top boards to the *inner* support (in about two and five-eighths inches from the ends).

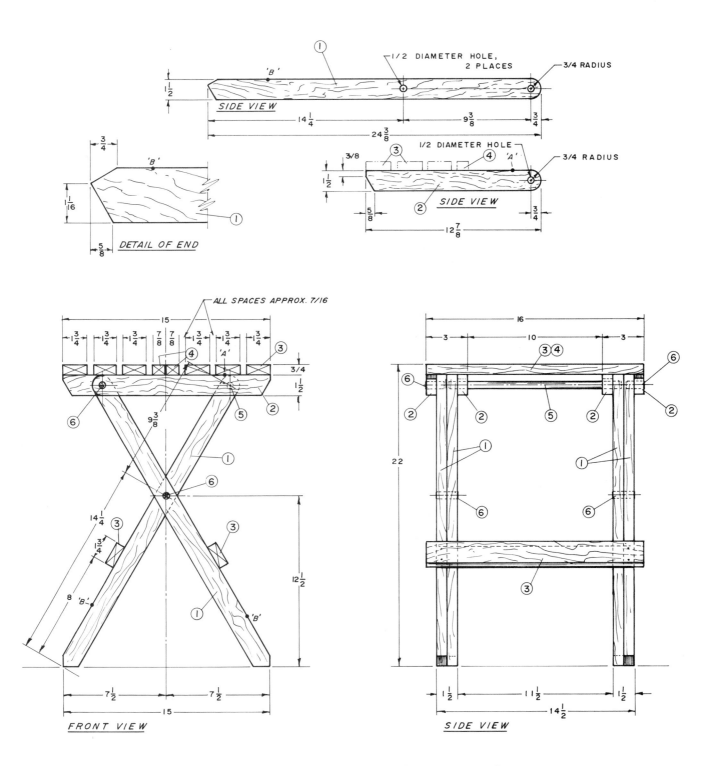

Nail the remaining top board, part no. 3, to the *inner* leg. Remove the spacers and *if* everything is correct, the table *should* fold out as shown in the front and side views.

Using a small drill bit, drill a hole through the legs and/or supports, into the center pin and short pins. Add a nail to lock the pins in place. If nails were used for the entire assembly, then set them and putty. Resand all over. Finish the table to your liking.

7♦Step Stool

Here is a weekend project *everyone* needs at one time or another. This step stool is sturdy and can also be used for a stool to sit on, especially with a small cushion or with the hinges recessed flush with the top. The step stool should be made of a hardwood. Ash or oak is an attractive, sturdy wood to use for this project.

Instructions

Cut all the pieces to overall size per the cutting list. Sand all over. Cut the four legs according to the given dimensions. Be sure that all four are exactly the same size and shape. I taped the four pieces of stock together with masking tape and then cut all the legs out together. Cut the 1/4-inch wide, 3/8-inch deep notch the entire length of the inner edge of each leg as shown.

Cut the bottom, center, and top supports to size with the ends slanting in at seven degrees as shown. Cut a tongue, or tenon, at each end that is 3/8-inch wide, 1/4-inch thick also slanting at seven degrees according to the plans. Dry-fit the two leg assemblies. Check that the top surface of the bottom support is 6 1/4 inches above the base. Check that the top surface of the center support is 13 1/4 inches above the base and that the top support fits correctly at the top. Adjust these pieces as necessary.

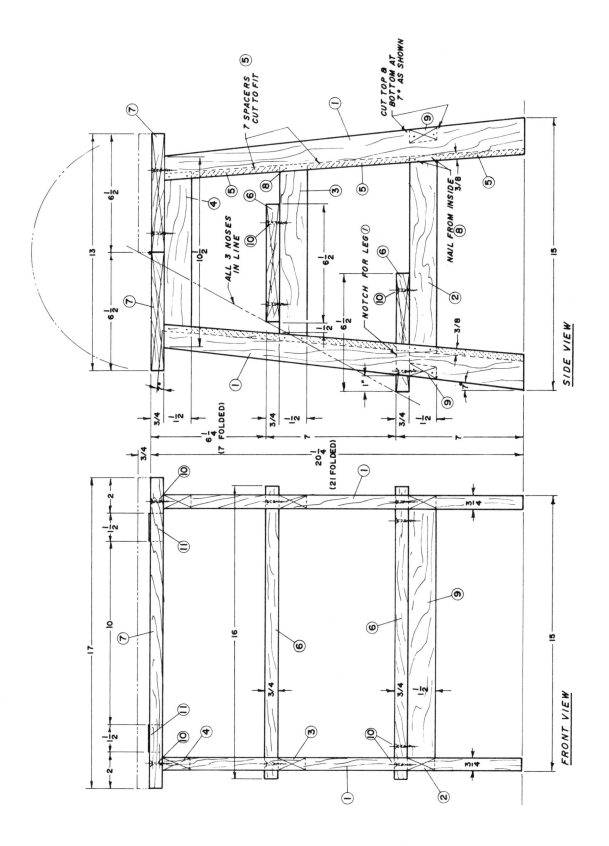

Glue and nail each leg subassembly together. Be sure both leg assemblies are exactly the same. Cut and fit the spacers; glue them in place for extra strength. Cut and fit the bottom step; glue and screw it in place. Check that it extends out one inch. Be sure everything is square. Add the middle step and the two braces. Again recheck for squareness. Add the hinges to the two top step pieces and fold one back over the other.

NO.	NAME	SIZE	REQ'D.
1	LEG	3/4 X 2 - 19 7/8 LG.	4
2	SUPPORT BOTTOM	3/4 X 1 1/2 - 11 LONG	2
3	SUPPORT CENTER	3/4 X 1 1/2 - 10 LONG	2
4	SUPPORT - TOP	3/4 X 1 1/2 - 9 LONG	2
5	SPACER ✳	1/4 X 5/16 - 72 LONG	1
6	STEP	3/4 X 6 1/2 - 16 LONG	2
7	STEP - TOP	3/4 X 6 1/2 - 17 LONG	2
8	NAIL - FINISH	4 d	24
9	BRACE	3/4 X 1 1/2 - 13 1/2 LG.	2
10	SCREW - FL. HD.	NO. 8 - 1 3/4 LONG	21
11	HINGE - BRASS	2 LONG	2

✳ CUT SPACER ⑤ TO FIT — 12 REQ'D.

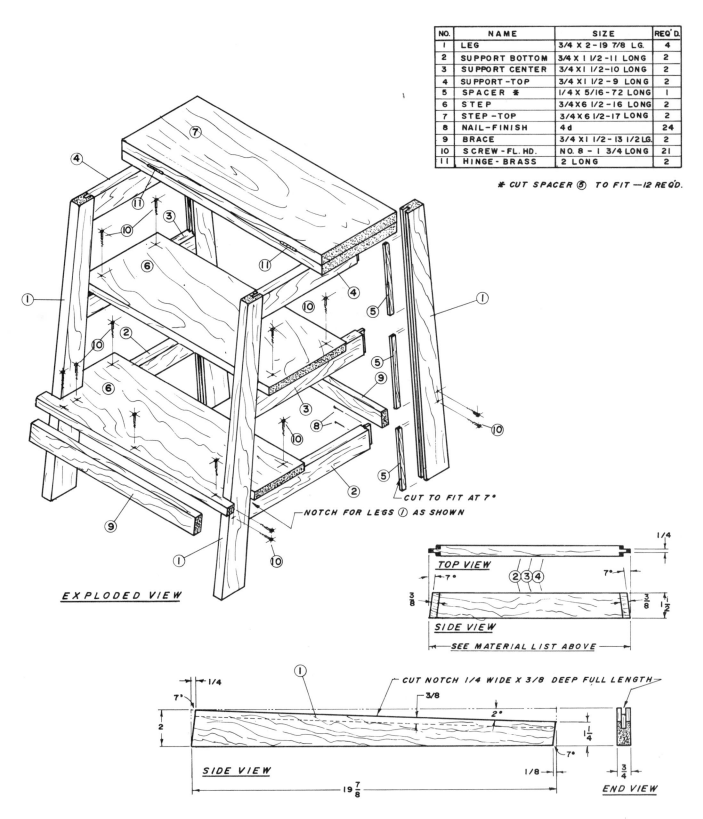

EXPLODED VIEW

CUT TO FIT AT 7°

NOTCH FOR LEGS ① AS SHOWN

TOP VIEW

SIDE VIEW

SEE MATERIAL LIST ABOVE

SIDE VIEW

CUT NOTCH 1/4 WIDE X 3/8 DEEP FULL LENGTH

END VIEW

Using a straight-edge board as a guide, line up the noses of the middle and bottom step with the *folded* top step as indicated in the side view drawing. This will locate the top step. Open the top step and screw the permanent side in place.

This project can be stained and varnished or painted.

8 ♦ Wall Shelf

This wall-shelf design is a takeoff of a design popular in the late thirties and early forties. Its size, as drawn, is just perfect for homes of today. The plans show blind dadoes for holding the shelves in place. If you do not have the tools required to make dadoes, you can simply eliminate them. The dadoes make a stronger shelf, but nailing the shelves in place will be adequate and strong enough. Without the dadoes, simply do not notch the ends of the shelves.

Instructions

Cut all the pieces to *overall* size, and sand all surfaces. On a sheet of heavy paper or cardboard, about six inches by 34 inches, draw a one-inch by one-inch grid. Transfer the shape of the side to the paper, point by point. Be sure to locate the three shelf locations and dadoes. On another sheet of heavy paper or cardboard, about six inches by 16 inches, draw another one-inch grid. Transfer the shape of the top scroll, point by point.

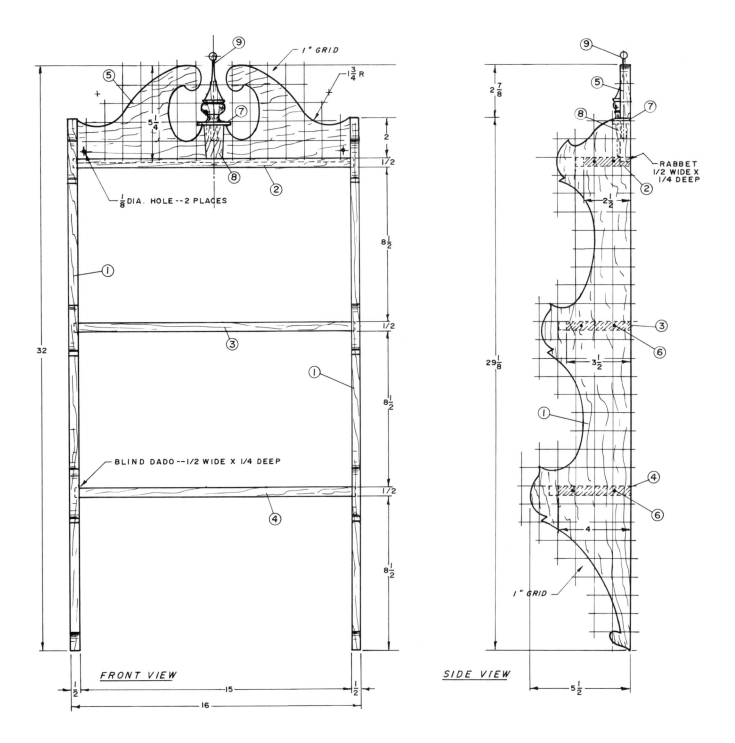

FRONT VIEW

SIDE VIEW

On each of the two side pieces locate and cut the three, 1/2-inch wide, 1/4-inch deep blind dadoes along with the 1/2-inch wide, 1/4-inch deep rabbet that is cut down from the top to meet the uppermost dado, as shown in the exploded view. Important: be sure to make a left- and right-hand *pair*. Line up each set of dadoes while you tape or tack the two side pieces together with the dadoes on the inside. Make sure that the three dadoes do line up exactly.

Locate the sites of the seven 6d nails for each side piece, as shown in the drawings. Drill a 1/16-inch diameter pilot hole at each location.

Transfer the pattern for the sides to the wood. With both pieces taped or tacked together, cut out the two sides. Sand all edges, taking care NOT to "round" any edges.

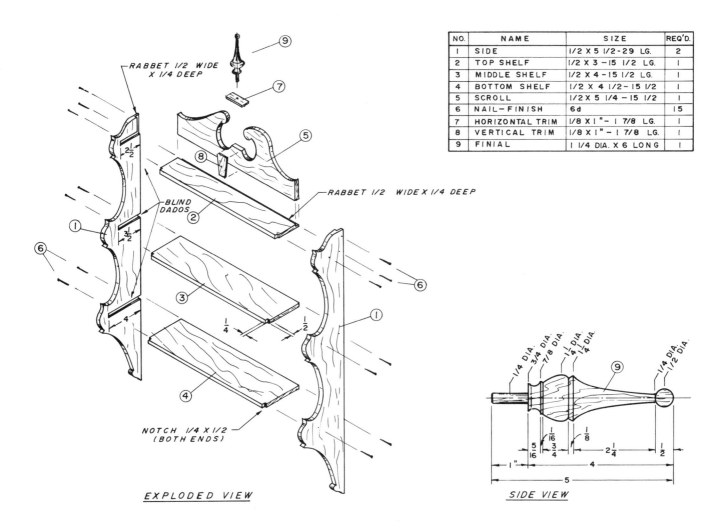

NO.	NAME	SIZE	REQ'D.
1	SIDE	1/2 X 5 1/2 - 29 LG.	2
2	TOP SHELF	1/2 X 3 - 15 1/2 LG.	1
3	MIDDLE SHELF	1/2 X 4 - 15 1/2 LG.	1
4	BOTTOM SHELF	1/2 X 4 1/2 - 15 1/2	1
5	SCROLL	1/2 X 5 1/4 - 15 1/2	1
6	NAIL - FINISH	6d	15
7	HORIZONTAL TRIM	1/8 X 1" - 1 7/8 LG.	1
8	VERTICAL TRIM	1/8 X 1" - 1 7/8 LG.	1
9	FINIAL	1 1/4 DIA. X 6 LONG	1

EXPLODED VIEW

SIDE VIEW

Transfer the top scroll pattern to the wood, and cut out the piece. Sand all edges. Make a 1/4-inch by 1/2-inch notch at the front edge of each shelf as shown in the exploded view, provided you were able to make the blind-dado cuts.

Dry-fit all of the pieces. If the dry assembly is okay, glue and nail the project together, taking care that all of the shelves are exactly 90 degrees to the sides.

Turn the piece for the finial as indicated in the drawing. If you do not have a lathe available, a purchased finial, approximately 1 1/4-inches in diameter and 4-inches long, will do. Try to select a finial similar in design to the drawing.

Add the horizontal and vertical trim. Drill a hole for the finial, and glue it in place.

Finishing

Sand all over. Stain and apply two, light top coats of varnish. Your shelf is ready for hanging. I added two, small brass hangers on the inside of the sides rather than drill the two, 1/8-inch diameter holes that are indicated on the front view drawing for the top scroll.

Your wall shelf is ready for displaying your favorite collection.

PROJECTS WITH A HEART

9 ◆ Wall Mirror

Here is a simple, small wall mirror that will brighten any child's room. The wood for the mirror can be of any kind and can be stained or painted to match the room.

Instructions

On a sheet of heavy paper or cardboard, about nine inches by 10 inches, draw a 1/2-inch grid. Lay out the two heart shapes, point by point. Also locate the indent for the mirror, measuring 4 7/8 inches by 5 5/8 inches.

Transfer the pattern for the two hearts to the wood, and carefully cut them out. Sand all edges. Using a router that has a bit with a ball-bearing follower, make the outer, 1/4-inch radius cove. Using the same bit with a ball-bearing follower, use the router to cut a 1/8-inch "round" along the inner heart.

Turn the heart over and locate the space for the mirror and backboard, approximately 4 7/8 inches by 5 5/8 inches. Cut out this space to a stepped-in depth of 5/8 of an inch.

Sand all over, and add the brass hanger.

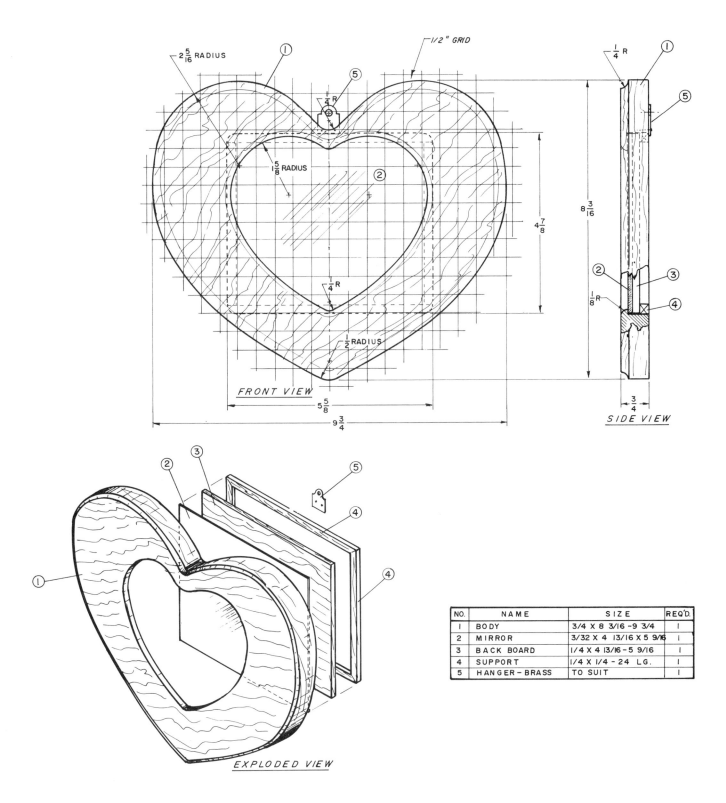

NO.	NAME	SIZE	REQ'D.
1	BODY	3/4 X 8 3/16 - 9 3/4	1
2	MIRROR	3/32 X 4 13/16 X 5 9/16	1
3	BACK BOARD	1/4 X 4 13/16 - 5 9/16	1
4	SUPPORT	1/4 X 1/4 - 24 LG.	1
5	HANGER - BRASS	TO SUIT	1

Finishing

Remove the brass hanger while you apply a finish. Use either stain or paint according to your preference. Insert the mirror and backboard. Tack the quarter-inch square supports in place to hold the mirror and backboard in place. The wall mirror is ready to hang in a lucky child's room or anywhere you like.

10 ♦ Wall Shelf with Mirror

Here is a simple project that combines a shelf with a small mirror. It is similar to project 9, the wall mirror, immediately prior to this. They are both made in exactly the same way. Simply follow the instructions for the wall mirror in making and finishing this project.

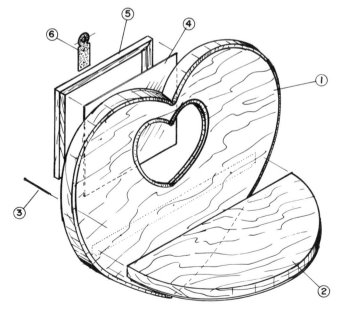

EXPLODED VIEW

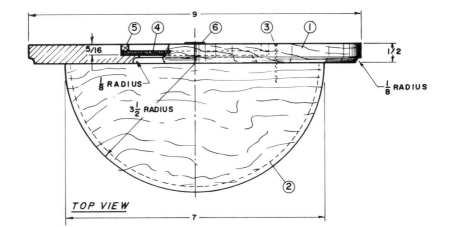

9

5/16

1/2

⅛ RADIUS

⅛ RADIUS

3½ RADIUS

⑤ ④ ⑥ ③ ①

②

TOP VIEW

7

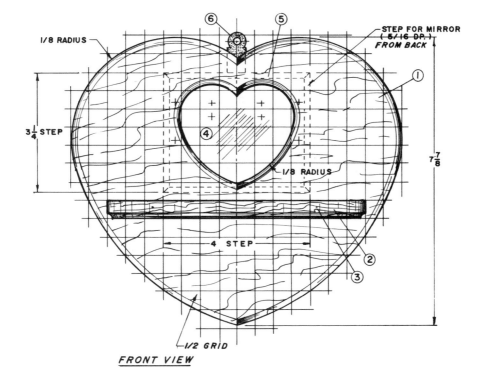

⑥ ⑤

1/8 RADIUS

STEP FOR MIRROR
(5/16 DP.)
FROM BACK

3¼ STEP

④

1/8 RADIUS

7⅞

①

4 STEP

②

③

1/2 GRID

FRONT VIEW

NO.	NAME	SIZE	REQ'D.
1	BASE	1/2 X 7 7/8 - 9 LONG	1
2	SHELF	1/2 X 3 1/2 - 7 LG.	1
3	FINISH NAIL	6 d	3
4	MIRROR	3/32 X 3 1/8 - 3 7/8	1
5	SUPPORT	1/8 X 1/8 - 16 LONG	1
6	BRASS HANGER	TO SUIT	1

41

11 ◆ Footstool

The design of this lovely footstool is intended to be a counterpart to the wall mirror and/or the wall shelf with mirror, projects 9 and 10. This project *should* be made of a hardwood so that it will hold up under all conditions. The footstool makes a great project for those who like rosemaling or tole painting (see the photograph for project 46, the milking stool).

Instructions

Draw a 1/2-inch grid on heavy paper or cardboard, and lay out the patterns for the seat, leg, and brace. On the seat pattern, locate the four screw holes.

Transfer the patterns to the wood, and cut them out. Note the two parallel, 15 degree cuts on the top and bottom ends of the two legs. Drill holes and countersink in the top and legs for the eight no. 8 screws.

Screw the stool together to check all fits, and make adjustments as necessary. When everything is alright, take the assembly completely apart again.

Using a router equipped with a 1/8-inch radius cove-cutter bit that has a ball-bearing follower, cut the outer edge of the top, the lower edge of the brace, and the outside edges of the two legs, as shown in the exploded view. Now you can apply glue and screw the stool together. Check that the stool is sturdy enough for all conditions. Now you are ready to finish this charming footstool as you desire.

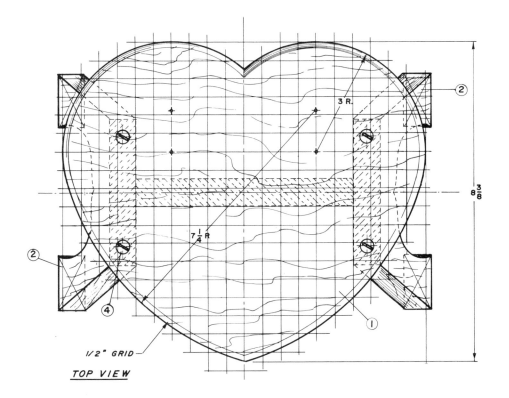

3 R.

②

8 $\frac{3}{8}$

②

④

7 $\frac{1}{4}$ R

①

1/2" GRID

TOP VIEW

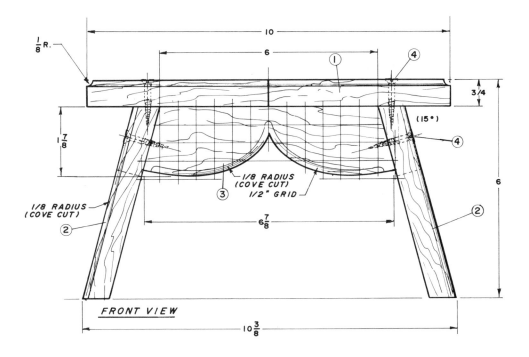

$\frac{1}{8}$ R.

10

6

①

④

3/4

(15°)

④

1 $\frac{7}{8}$

1/8 RADIUS
(COVE CUT)

1/2" GRID

③

6

1/8 RADIUS
(COVE CUT)

②

6 $\frac{7}{8}$

②

FRONT VIEW

10 $\frac{3}{8}$

NO.	NAME	SIZE	REQ'D.
1	SEAT	3/4 X 8 3/8—10 LG.	1
2	LEG	3/4 X 6 1/2—5 5/8	2
3	BRACE	3/4 X 1 7/8—6 7/8	1
4	SCREW FLAT HEAD	NO. 8—1 1/4 LONG	8

43

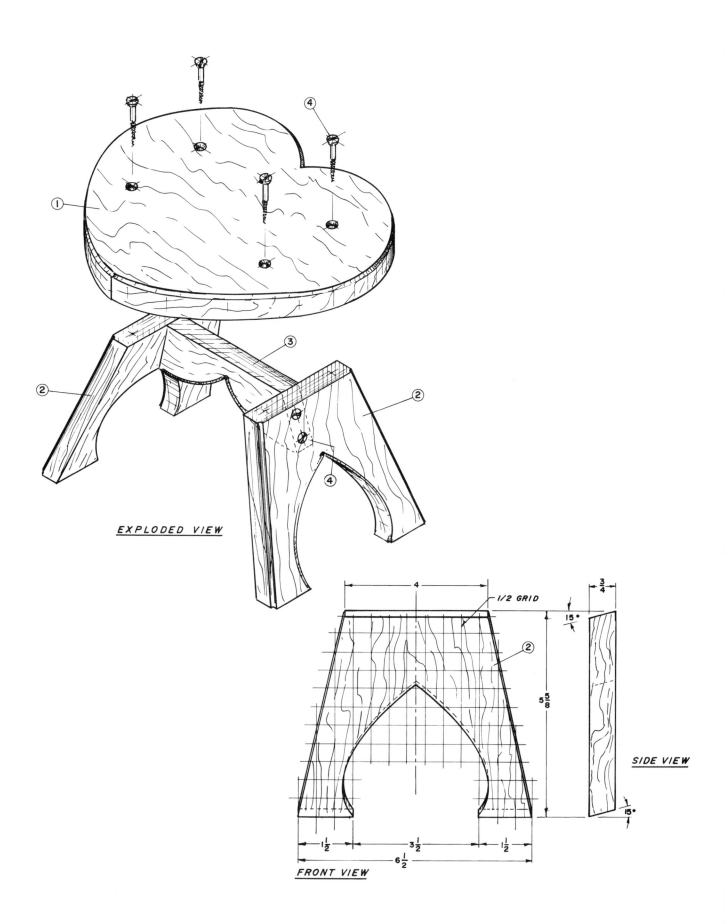

EXPLODED VIEW

1/2 GRID

SIDE VIEW

FRONT VIEW

12 ◆ Child's Bench

This bench is a scaled-down version of a sleigh bench that was once used for an extra seat in a horse-drawn open sleigh years ago. These slightly decorated sleigh benches were especially popular in Pennsylvania. Today this smaller version makes an excellent bench for a child's room. This project can be made of either soft or hard wood as its design produces a very sturdy construction.

Instructions

Cut all the pieces to overall size, and sand all edges. Lay out the patterns for the ends and skirt. Transfer the patterns to the wood, and cut them out.

Using a router bit with a 1/8-inch radius cove-cutter and ball-bearing follower, rout the top edge of the ends, the arched leg sections, and the seat, as shown in the drawings.

Locate and attach the seat supports to the ends. Glue and screw these in place. Note: the supports should be three-quarters of an inch *in* from each side. Glue the skirt pieces and seat to the ends. Check that everything is square.

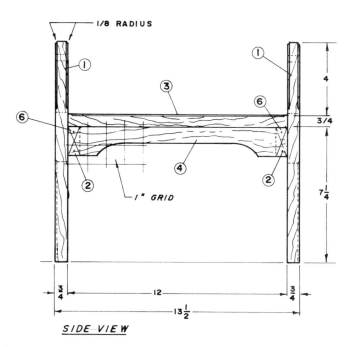

1/8 RADIUS

③

⑥

⑥

3/4

④

2

1" GRID

⑥

2

4

7¼

3/4

12

3/4

13½

SIDE VIEW

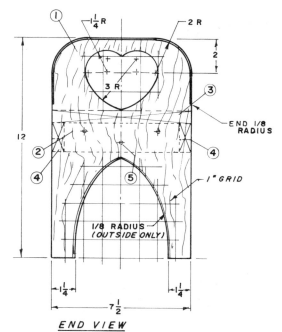

①

1¼ R

2 R

2

3 R

③

END 1/8 RADIUS

12

2

②

④

④

⑤

1" GRID

1/8 RADIUS (OUTSIDE ONLY)

1¼

7½

1¼

END VIEW

NO.	NAME	SIZE	REQ'D.
1	END	3/4 X 7 1/2 - 12 LONG	2
2	SUPPORT	3/4 X 1 1/2 - 5 3/4 LG.	2
3	SEAT	3/4 X 7 1/2 - 12 LONG	1
4	SKIRT	3/4 X 1 1/2 - 12 LONG	2
5	SCREW - FL. HD.	NO. 8 - 1 1/4 LONG	6
6	FINISH NAIL	6 d	14

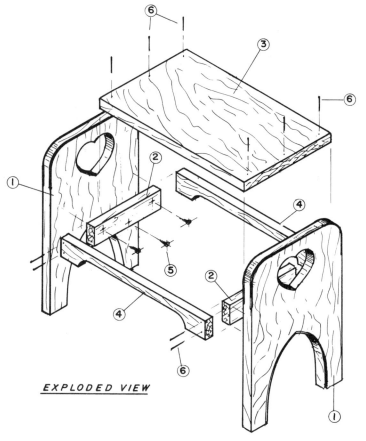

EXPLODED VIEW

Finishing

Finish to match the room in which you will put this bench, if possible.

13 ◆ Bread Basket

This project has all kind of uses and can be made of any softwood. Stained or painted it will make an appealing addition wherever it is used.

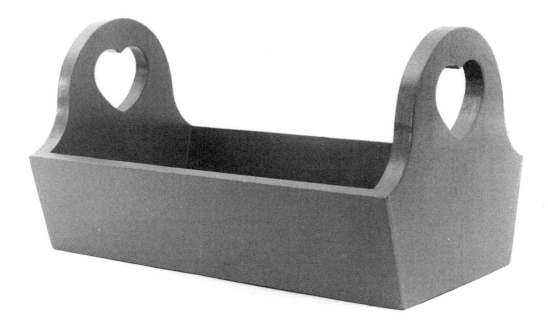

Instructions

Cut all the parts to size per the cutting list. Make a full-size pattern for the ends, and transfer the pattern to the wood. Tape two pieces of stock together with the pattern in place and cut out both end pieces at once. Sand all edges while they are still taped together so that the two ends will match exactly.

Cut a 1/2-inch wide, 1/8-inch deep rabbet on both ends of the side pieces. Set your saw at 15 degrees, and cut the *bottom* edge of the sides at this setting so that the inclined edge will be flush with the bottom piece when assembled.

Also cut the two side edges of the bottom piece at 15 degrees. It is a good idea to fit the bottom piece *after* the ends and sides are assembled to allow for some adjustments due to variation in construction. Glue and nail the complete assembly, and finish to your liking.

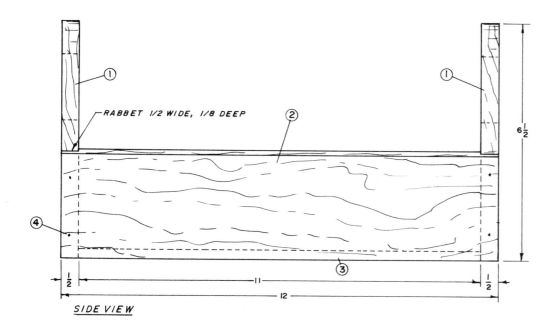

RABBET 1/2 WIDE, 1/8 DEEP

①

②

③

④

6½

½   11   ½

12

SIDE VIEW

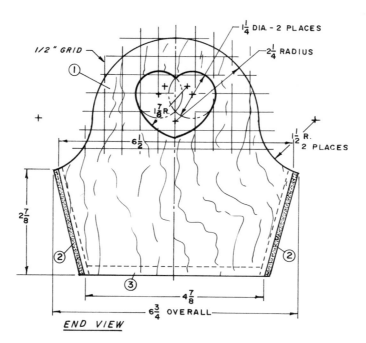

1/2" GRID

1¼ DIA - 2 PLACES

2¼ RADIUS

①

7/8 R.

1½ R.
2 PLACES

6½

2⅞

②   ②

③

4⅞

6¾ OVERALL

END VIEW

NO.	NAME	SIZE	REQ'D.
1	END	1/2 X 6 1/2 - 6 1/2 LG.	2
2	SIDE	1/4 X 3 - 12 LONG	2
3	BOTTOM	1/4 X 4 13/16 - 11 LG.	1
4	BRAD	1/2 LONG	8

48

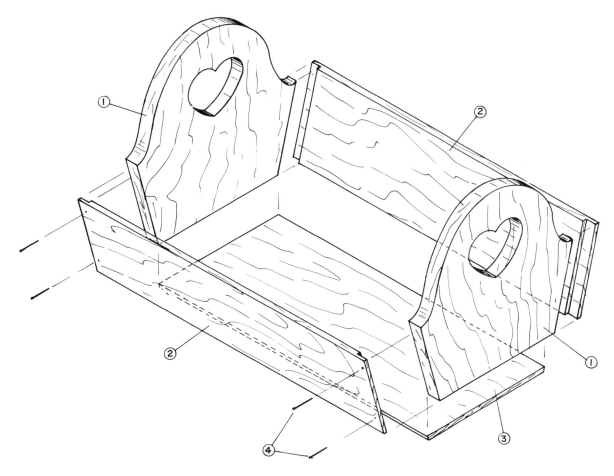

EXPLODED VIEW

49

14 ◆ Garden Caddy

This is a project that can be used for all kinds of things. It can be made of any kind of wood, but it just "cries out" for oak or ash. If you have never worked with oak or ash, this project is the *perfect* time to try it.

Instructions

Make full-size patterns for the ends and sides on a piece of cardboard. Tape or tack two pieces of stock together, and cut both ends out together. Drill the 7/8-inch diameter hole at this time. Sand the edges while the end pieces are still taped or tacked together to ensure that the two ends are *exactly* the same size. Do the same for the two sides.

Finishing

Glue and nail the caddy together, and sand all over. The caddy can be stained or painted. If you used oak or ash, then finish your caddy similar to the two versions pictured by simply applying a top coat of tough, clear finish.

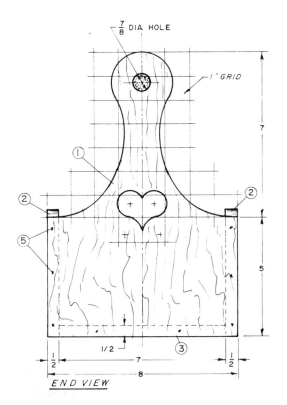

$\frac{7}{8}$ DIA. HOLE

1" GRID

① ②

② ②

⑤

1/2

1/2

1/2

7

8

7

5

END VIEW

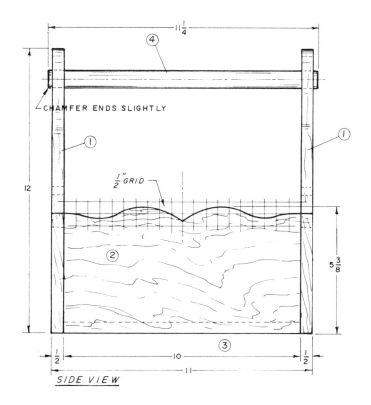

11 $\frac{1}{4}$

④

CHAMFER ENDS SLIGHTLY

① ①

12

$\frac{1}{2}$" GRID

②

5 $\frac{3}{8}$

1/2

10

11

③

SIDE VIEW

NO.	NAME	SIZE	REQ'D.
1	END	1/2 X 7 - 12 LONG	2
2	SIDE	1/2 X 5 3/8 - 10 LONG	2
3	BOTTOM	1/2 X 7 - 10 LONG	1
4	HANDLE - DOWEL	7/8 DIA. X 11 1/4 LG.	1
5	NAIL - FINISH	6 d	16

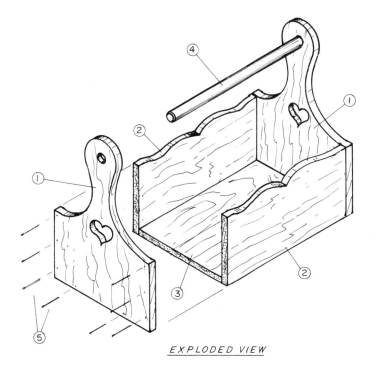

④

② ①

① ②

③

⑤

EXPLODED VIEW

51

15 ♦ Corner Shelf

Shelves usually are designed to hang along a wall; well, why not in the *corner*? This shelf will fit snugly into an empty corner and provide an excellent place to display all kinds of things.

Instructions

Make a full-size pattern of the front. Transfer the pattern to the wood, and cut it out. Be sure to cut the ends at 45 degrees as shown in the top view. Carefully lay out the shelf. Take care to get a 90 degree angle in the corner, but don't cut it yet. Using whatever bit or bits you have, rout the front edge of the shelf. If you do not have the exact cutters to produce the front edge detail, whatever detail you can manage is fine. If you do not have a router, leave the front of the shelf plain or square.

The 3/8-inch wide, 3/16-inch deep dado is optional; cut that at this time if you want it. *After* cutting the dado and routing the front edge, make the two 45 degree cuts to form an exact 90 degree angle. Slightly "round" the tip of the 90 degree angle so that the shelf will fit into the corner without hurting the wall. Make up the two brackets. Then in each bracket drill pilot holes and countersink for two, no. 8 flathead screws.

Finishing

Nail and glue the corner shelf together, and sand all over. Stain and paint as you desire.

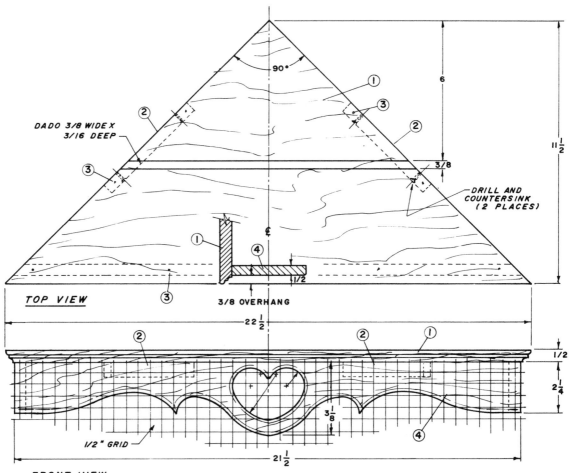

90°

DADO 3/8 WIDE X
3/16 DEEP

6

11 1/2

3/8

DRILL AND
COUNTERSINK
(2 PLACES)

1/2

TOP VIEW

3/8 OVERHANG

22 1/2

1/2

2 1/4

3/8

1/2" GRID

21 1/2

FRONT VIEW

NO.	NAME	SIZE	REQ'D.
1	SHELF	1/2 X 11 1/4 - 22 1/2	1
2	BRACKET	1/2 X 3/4 - 5 LONG	2
3	NAIL FINISH	4d	8
4	FRONT	1/2 X 3 1/8 - 21 1/2	1

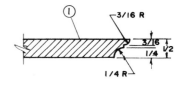

3/16 R

3/16

1/2

1/4

1/4 R

FRONT EDGE DETAIL

EXPLODED VIEW

16 ♦ Child's Swedish Sled

For those woodworkers who live in a snowbelt and have young children or grandchildren, this sled is just perfect. For those from warmer climes, it will make a great decorative piece or you could use it to put your plants on. Any kind of wood can be used, but oak or ash would be best. Your sled can be left plain, as the one pictured, or could be painted. A project such as this one makes a great tole painting or rosemaling project.

Instructions

Cut all the wood to overall size. Be sure to order and have on hand the spindle or other purchased turning for the pull before starting. As these turnings vary in length slightly from vendor to vendor, you may have to trim the length to hold the 10 1/4-inch dimension shown in the top view.

Tape or tack the two pieces of stock together and transfer the pattern for the runners to the top board. Locate and drill a 1/16-inch diameter hole where the larger hole for the pull (spindle) will be drilled. Locate and cut out the two 3/4-inch by 3/4-inch notches for the two braces. Cut out the remaining shape. While the two runners are still taped or tacked together, sand all edges. You should have an exact pair of runners. Separate the two runners and *on the inside* surface of both runners, drill a blind hole for the pull, 5/8-inch deep. Use the small, 1/16-inch diameter hole to locate each larger hole and to ensure that both holes line up exactly.

Be careful to start on the inside, and do not drill all the way through!

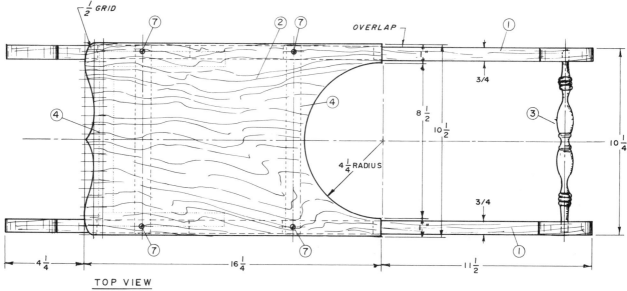

TOP VIEW
(SHOWN WITHOUT PARTS ⑤⑥ & ⑧ IN PLACE)

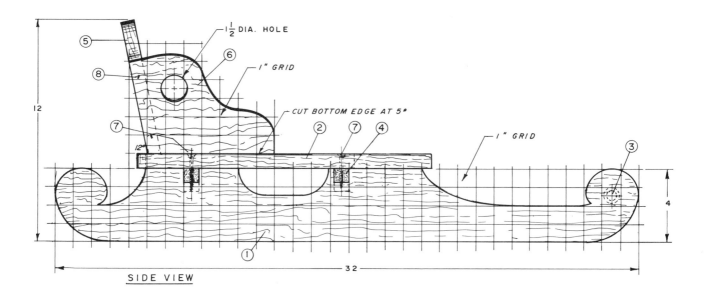

SIDE VIEW

Lay out the seat. *If* your spindle or pull is too long, you will either have to trim it or widen the seat. Be sure to check this before you cut the seat to the 10 1/4-inch width.

Cut the seat to size, and drill and countersink holes for the four flathead screws. Cut out two matching braces as indicated in the drawing. Sand all pieces, taking care not to "round" any edges.

Dry-fit all the parts, and adjust if necessary. If okay, glue the two braces and the pull to the two runners keeping everything square. Glue and screw the seat in place. If hardwood is used, predrill for the four screws so that the wood will not split.

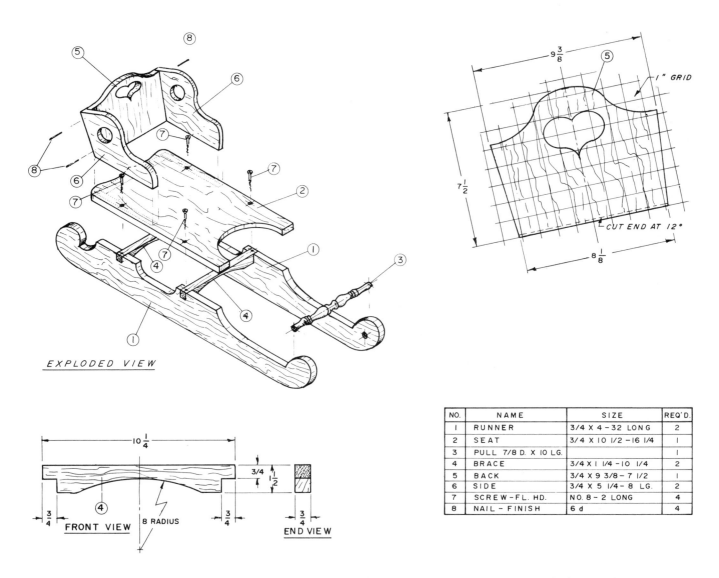

EXPLODED VIEW

FRONT VIEW

8 RADIUS

END VIEW

10 1/4

3/4

1 1/2

3/4

3/4

3/4

9 3/8

1" GRID

7 1/2

CUT END AT 12°

8 1/8

NO.	NAME	SIZE	REQ'D.
1	RUNNER	3/4 X 4 – 32 LONG	2
2	SEAT	3/4 X 10 1/2 – 16 1/4	1
3	PULL	7/8 D. X 10 LG.	1
4	BRACE	3/4 X 1 1/4 – 10 1/4	2
5	BACK	3/4 X 9 3/8 – 7 1/2	1
6	SIDE	3/4 X 5 1/4 – 8 LG.	2
7	SCREW – FL. HD.	NO. 8 – 2 LONG	4
8	NAIL – FINISH	6 d	4

Carefully cut the *bottom* edge of the two sides at about six degrees. Lay out the pattern and cut the two sides while the two pieces are taped or tacked together so that both sides will be an exact pair—*exactly* the same. Locate and drill the 1 1/2-inch diameter holes. Separate the parts and sand all over.

Lay out the shape of the back. Make the 12 degree cut across the bottom edge first. Then cut out the shape of the back, and sand all over. Glue the two sides and back together. Drill and fasten with finishing nails for added strength *after* the glue sets. Note: if you are going to use the sled in the snow, be sure to use waterproof glue.

Check that the *bottom* surface of the two sides and back are perfectly flat after assembly. If not, sand so that the three parts will sit flush on a smooth flat surface. Locate and glue the sides and back in place.

Finishing

Sand all over, and now you *can* round all exposed edges slightly. Finish to your liking. All you need is a snowstorm.

FOLK ART PROJECTS

17◆Dr. Hex on a Stick

Folk Art projects, such as this are becoming very popular. As illustrated this one is about 15 1/2-inches long. If you want yours to be a smaller size, simply use a smaller grid in laying out your pattern. Adjust the size of the stand accordingly. A 3/8-inch grid will reduce the figure to about 11 1/2-inches long, and a 1/4-inch grid will reduce it by half to 7 3/4-inches long. Be sure to reduce the thickness, also. Use 3/4-inch thick wood for the full-size figure, 9/16-inch thick wood for the 11 1/2-inch length, and 3/8-inch thick wood for the 7 3/4-inch length.

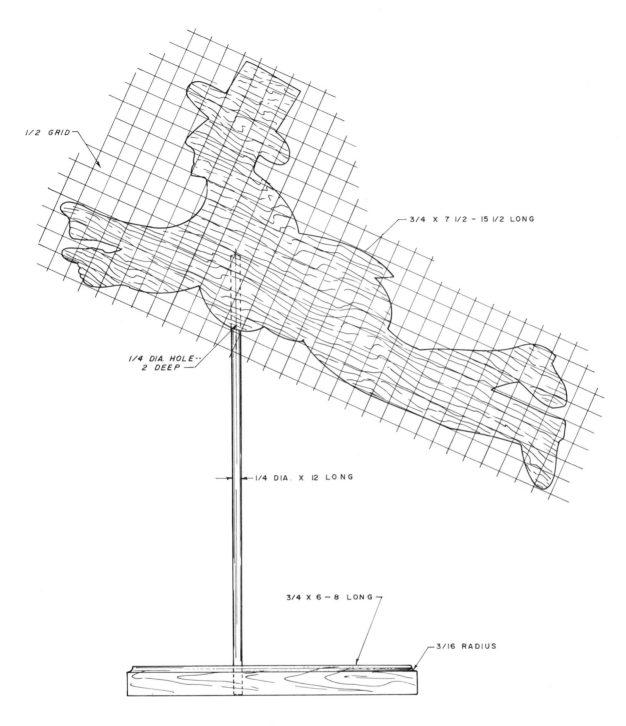

1/2 GRID

3/4 X 7 1/2 – 15 1/2 LONG

1/4 DIA. HOLE
2 DEEP

1/4 DIA. X 12 LONG

3/4 X 6 – 8 LONG

3/16 RADIUS

Instructions

Lay out the pattern on heavy cardboard, and cut it out. Note: be sure to locate the hole for the support on the pattern. Using the cardboard as a template, transfer the pattern to the wood. Cut the figure out of the wood, and sand all edges. Drill the hole for the support in both the body and the base.

Finishing

Assemble the figure and stand and finish as you wish.

18 ♦ Cock Weather Vane

America's true Folk Art started with weather vanes. They came in all shapes and sizes, some very elaborate, others very crude. I would say, this one is somewhat on the crude side, *but* it does have "character." At first glance, don't dismiss this project; it sells well at craft fairs here in New England. The one pictured has been "weathered" with a torch; some details were burned off in the process, if you compare it to the pattern. This project can also be reduced by using a smaller grid in laying out the pattern.

Instructions

Lay out the pattern on heavy paper on cardboard. Transfer the pattern to the wood, and cut the design out. Drill for the 1/4-inch diameter support in both the body and the base.

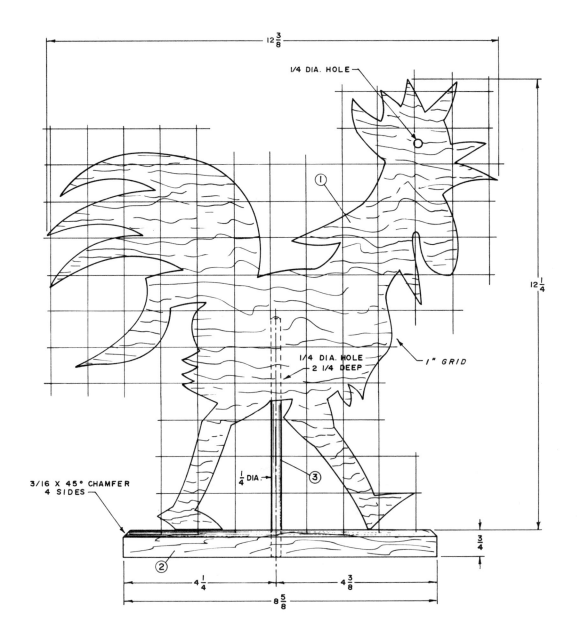

NO.	NAME	SIZE	REQ'D.
1	BODY	5/8 X 12 1/4 - 12 3/8	1
2	BASE	3/4 X 3 - 8 5/8 LG.	1
3	SUPPORT	1/4 DIA. X 6 1/2 LG.	1

Finishing

Finish to suit, but this makes a great project for experimenting to get a believable old look. Use a propane torch to "weather" your weather vane. Then, using a steel brush, remove all burned wood. Finally, lightly paint your weather vane with a thinned-out coat of grey paint. Now your Folk Art weather vane has that 100-year old "weathered" look.

20 ♦ Nutcracker Horse and Rider Toy

My daughter, Joy, collects all kinds of toy rocking horses. This one is very different from all the others in her collection. It is a fun project to make. Let your imagination loose, and paint it as you wish—as *you* think a nutcracker should look. I would suggest that you make two or three of these at the same time, since everyone who sees it will want one.

Instructions

Cut all the flat parts to shape, and sand them all over. Drill all holes as shown. The body and arms will have to be turned on a lathe.

Assemble the rocker and two rocker trim pieces with glue. After the glue sets, sand along the bottom 2 1/2-inch radius curve. Glue the hat brim and nose to the body. Glue the body legs and horse's head to the rocker subassembly. Allow to set, and *temporarily* add the arms with small brads to check for fit.

Finishing

Remove the arms after you are sure of the fit, and prime all parts. For speed, I recommend using fast-drying, easy-cleanup latex paint. Apply the top coats of paint using the suggested colors or colors you prefer. You can paint a "smiling" face if you wish, as my wife did.

After all the painting is done, reattach the arms with glue and brads. Attach the gold twine to the hat, and run string from one hand through the 1/16-inch diameter hole in the horse's head to the other hand. This completes your nutcracker rocking horse. Take care that he doesn't ride off into the sunset.

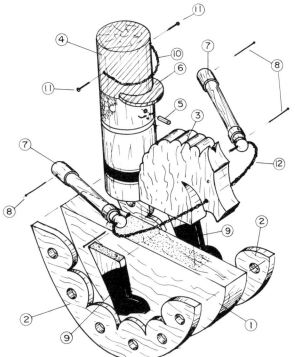

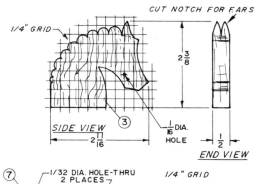

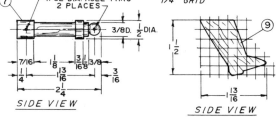

CUT NOTCH FOR EARS

1/4" GRID

2 3/8

SIDE VIEW
2 11/16

3

1/16 DIA. HOLE

END VIEW
1/2

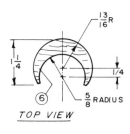

7 — 1/32 DIA. HOLE-THRU 2 PLACES

3/8 D. 1/2 DIA.

1/4" GRID

9

1 1/2

SIDE VIEW
1 13/16

7/16 1 1/8 3 3/16 3/8
1/4 1 13/16 3/16
2 1/4

SIDE VIEW

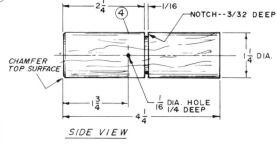

2 1/4 1/16

4 NOTCH--3/32 DEEP

CHAMFER TOP SURFACE

1 1/4 DIA.

1 3/4

1/16 DIA. HOLE 1/4 DEEP

4 1/4

SIDE VIEW

13/16 R

1 1/4 1/4

6 5/8 RADIUS

TOP VIEW

NO.	NAME	SIZE	REQ'D.
I	ROCKER	3/4 X 2 1/2 – 5 LG.	1
2	ROCKER TRIM	1/4 X 2 1/2 – 5 LG.	2
3	HEAD	1/2 X 2 11/16 – 2 3/8	1
4	BODY	1 1/4 DIA. – 4 1/4 LG.	1
5	NOSE	1/16 DIA. – 7/16 LG.	1
6	HAT BRIM	1/16 X 1 1/4 – 1 5/8	1
7	ARM	1/2 DIA. – 2 1/4 LG.	1
8	BRAD	1 1/4 LONG	4
9	LEG	1/4 X 1 13/16 – 1 1/2	2
10	TWINE (GOLD)	1 1/2 LONG	1
11	TACK (BRASS)	1/2 LONG	2
12	STRING (RED)	4 LONG	5

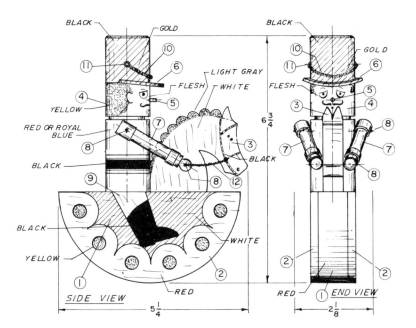

BLACK GOLD BLACK

LIGHT GRAY
FLESH WHITE
FLESH

RED OR ROYAL BLUE

YELLOW

BLACK

BLACK
YELLOW

RED

SIDE VIEW
5 1/4

WHITE

GOLD

RED END VIEW
2 1/8

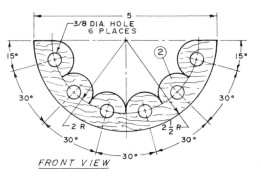

5

2 1/2 RADIUS

FRONT VIEW

5

3/8 DIA. HOLE 6 PLACES

15° 15°
30° 30°
2 R 2 1/2 R
30° 30° 30°

FRONT VIEW

64

21◆Cranberry Scoop (Wall Mail Holder)

I don't think you will need one of these to go out and harvest a crop of cranberries, but hanging it on the wall creates all kinds of possibilities. It makes a great wall box for outgoing mail, for plants, a place to store candles or whatever you can imagine using it for.

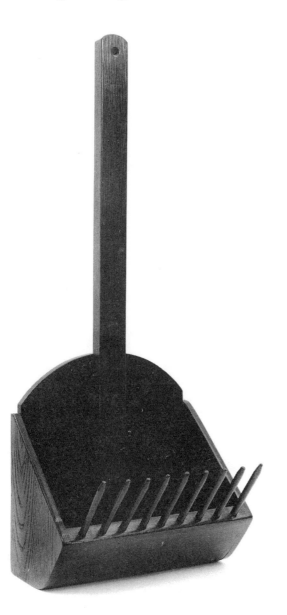

Instructions

Cut all the parts to size. Make a 50 degree cut on the bottom piece, as shown in the side view. On the front piece, locate and drill the nine, 1/4-inch diameter holes for the fingers. Start the first and last holes *in* three-quarters of an inch, then one inch apart, as shown. Also make a 50 degree cut on the bottom edge of the front. Glue the front and bottom together. "Round" the front edge of the bottom as shown in the side view.

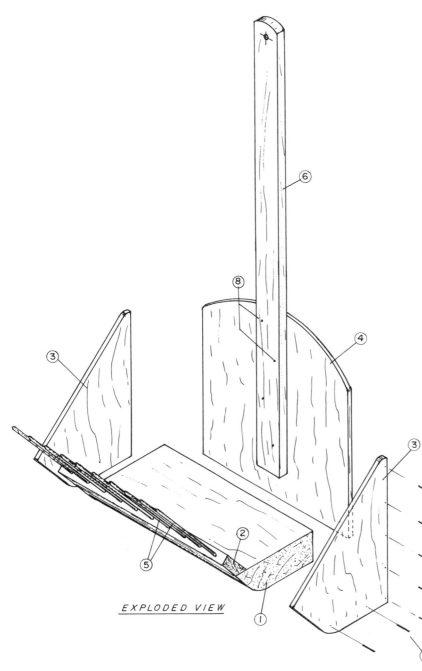

NO.	NAME	SIZE	REQ'D.
1	BOTTOM	1 5/8 X 5 – 9 1/2 LG.	1
2	FRONT	3/4 X 2 1/8 – 9 1/2 LG	1
3	SIDE	1/4 X 6 – 8 LONG	2
4	BACK	1/4 X 9 1/2 – 10 1/2 LG	1
5	FINGERS	1/4 DIA. – 4 1/2 LG	9
6	HANDLE	3/4 X 1 1/2 – 24 3/8	1
7	SQUARE CUT NAIL	3/4 LONG	14
8	SQUARE CUT NAIL	1 LONG	4

EXPLODED VIEW

Lay out the pattern for the two sides, and cut them out. Sand all over. Note: the lower and forward side should match the front and bottom sub-assembly. Cut out the back, and sand all over.

Make up the handle according to the plans. Attach the two sides and back to the front and bottom assembly using glue and nails. Attach the handle, and your assembly is done.

Finishing

Stain or paint as you choose. Your versatile wall-box scoop is ready for hanging.

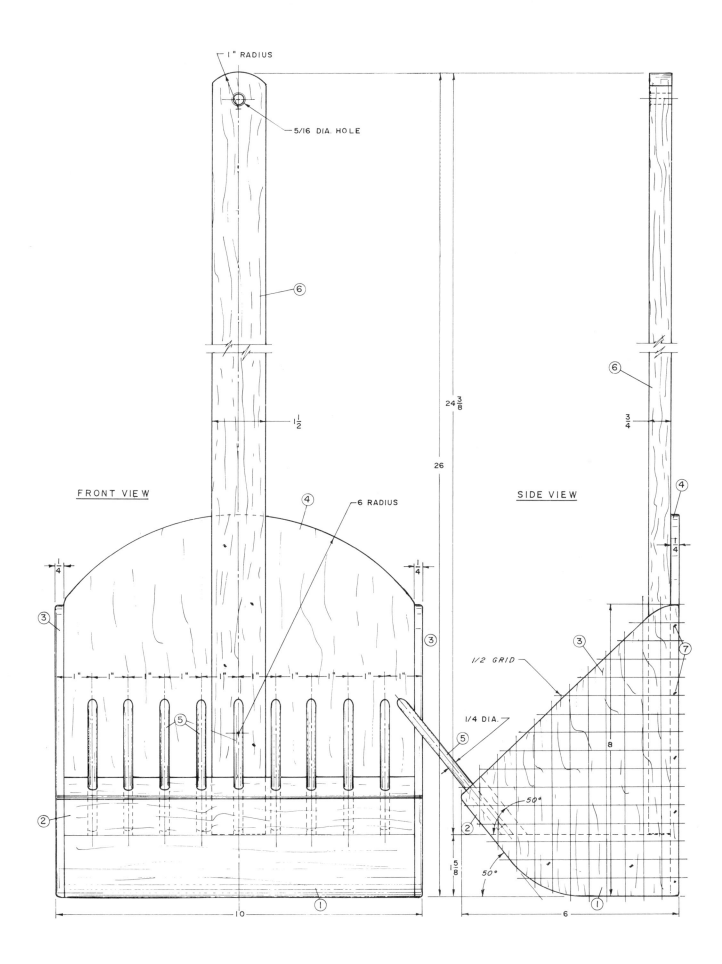

1" RADIUS

5/16 DIA. HOLE

24 $\frac{3}{8}$

26

1 $\frac{1}{2}$

FRONT VIEW

6 RADIUS

$\frac{1}{4}$

$\frac{1}{4}$

1" 1" 1" 1" 1" 1" 1" 1" 1"

10

SIDE VIEW

$\frac{3}{4}$

$\frac{1}{4}$

1/2 GRID

1/4 DIA.

8

50°

5 $\frac{5}{8}$

50°

6

67

22♦Small Wheelbarrow Planters With Boy and Girl Figures

This is the kind of project that was very popular in the early forties. Today they are "collectables." As a kid, I can remember most everyone made small projects such as these and displayed them proudly around the house.

I found these two particular "workers" at a flea market and would guess that they are from this period. My newly purchased "collectables" were in bad shape, but enough was left to create a pattern and redraw the plans.

They are brightly colored and will add a lot to your plants. You can make one or the other or both, if you choose.

Instructions

Lay out all the parts full size on a sheet of heavy paper or cardboard. Be sure to note the location of all holes. Transfer the pattern and hole locations to the wood. Cut out all the pieces according to the plans. Don't forget to make a saw kerf to divide the legs of the figures.

To make up the wheelbarrow, glue the bottom and front together, then attach the two sides. Sand all over when the glue sets. Make up the left- and right-hand handle. Make up the wheel and attach the two handles *with the wheel temporarily attached.* Add the two legs and the wheelbarrow is done, ready for painting.

To make the figures, simply attach the arms to the body. To get the exact position of the arms, temporarily attach the hands to the wheelbarrow. Check that the wheelbarrow and feet are resting flush on the surface. Note: you will have to trim the handles of the wheelbarrow and the hands slightly to get the proper fit. The originals had the arms set at a slight angle.

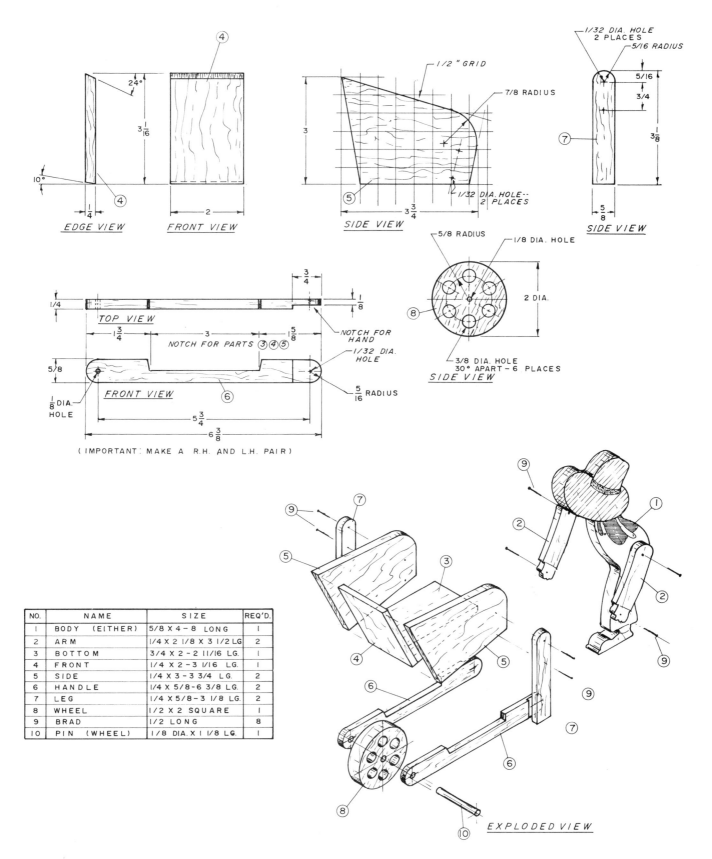

NO.	NAME	SIZE	REQ'D.
1	BODY (EITHER)	5/8 X 4 - 8 LONG	1
2	ARM	1/4 X 2 1/8 X 3 1/2 LG	2
3	BOTTOM	3/4 X 2 - 2 11/16 LG.	1
4	FRONT	1/4 X 2 - 3 1/16 LG.	1
5	SIDE	1/4 X 3 - 3 3/4 LG.	2
6	HANDLE	1/4 X 5/8 - 6 3/8 LG.	2
7	LEG	1/4 X 5/8 - 3 1/8 LG.	2
8	WHEEL	1/2 X 2 SQUARE	1
9	BRAD	1/2 LONG	8
10	PIN (WHEEL)	1/8 DIA. X 1 1/8 LG.	1

Finishing

Separate the wheel and hands from the wheelbarrow, and prime all of the parts. Using fast-drying latex paint, paint the features similar to what is shown in the plans. Use your imagination as you wish.

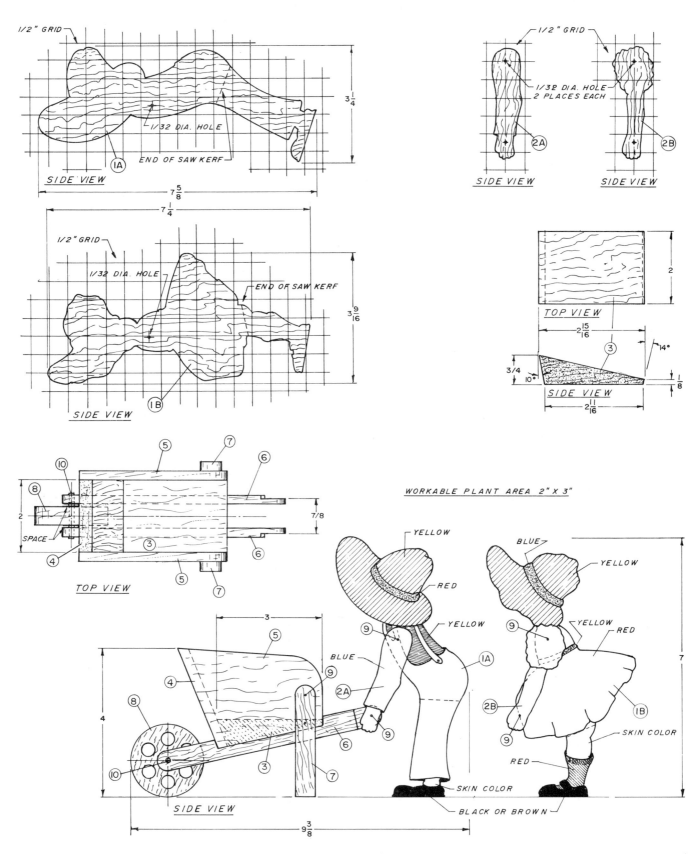

The colors called off in the plans are the colors used on the originals I purchased, but *any* color combination can be used. Permanently reattach the wheel and hands to the wheelbarrow. Make sure the feet rest squarely on the surface before the glue sets.

Add a small plant and you're back in the forties.

23 ◆ Wall Shelf

This project is especially for any woodworker with a scroll saw that is one of the new parallel-arm models. This project and the next were popular in the early thirties but seem to be coming back. I found the original of this one in an antiques shop on Martha's Vineyard, a few summers ago. The antiques dealer dated it in the late twenties. These two projects are a little time consuming, but a lot of fun to make. You should use a straight-grain hardwood for projects such as these. Walnut is a very good choice and cuts nicely. Most of the wall shelves of this vintage were made of walnut.

Instructions

Draw a midline down the middle of a sheet of paper that is about ten inches by sixteen inches. On the *left* side of the midline, draw a 1/2-inch grid. Carefully transfer the design to the left side, point by point. Be sure to locate the hole called off as "A," and the holes called off as "B." Note the location of the shelf, brace, and the 1/4-inch diameter hole. Fold the paper along the midline and cut out the pattern. This will ensure that you have a pattern that is exactly the same size and shape but reversed on either side of the midline.

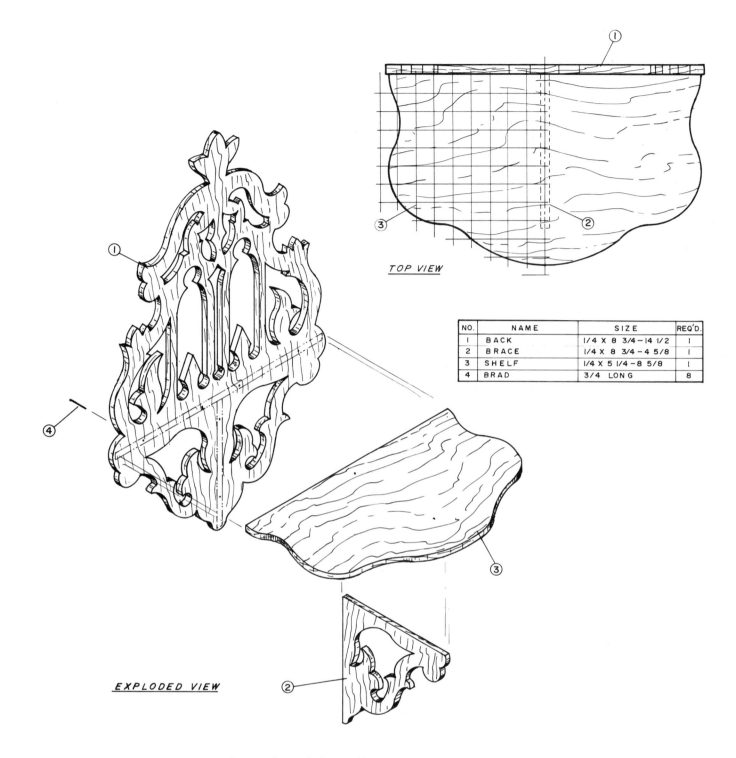

TOP VIEW

NO.	NAME	SIZE	REQ'D.
1	BACK	1/4 X 8 3/4 – 14 1/2	1
2	BRACE	1/4 X 8 3/4 – 4 5/8	1
3	SHELF	1/4 X 5 1/4 – 8 5/8	1
4	BRAD	3/4 LONG	8

EXPLODED VIEW

Cut and sand the surfaces of all the pieces. Glue the paper pattern to the wood using rubber cement or removable spray mount. Locate and drill the two 3/4-inch diameter holes as noted by "A." Locate and drill the nine 1/2-inch diameter holes as noted by "B." Locate and drill the nine 1/2-inch diameter holes as noted by "B." Drill the 1/4″ diameter hole and countersink it slightly to give it a "finished" look.

Carefully cut out the back, following as close as possible to the pattern. If you do get off a little, try to do the same thing on the opposite side. Remember, this does not have to be exact; if you do stray here and there, no one will ever know once you remove the pattern. The "original" piece I purchased must have been cut out by hand as it was *very* crude.

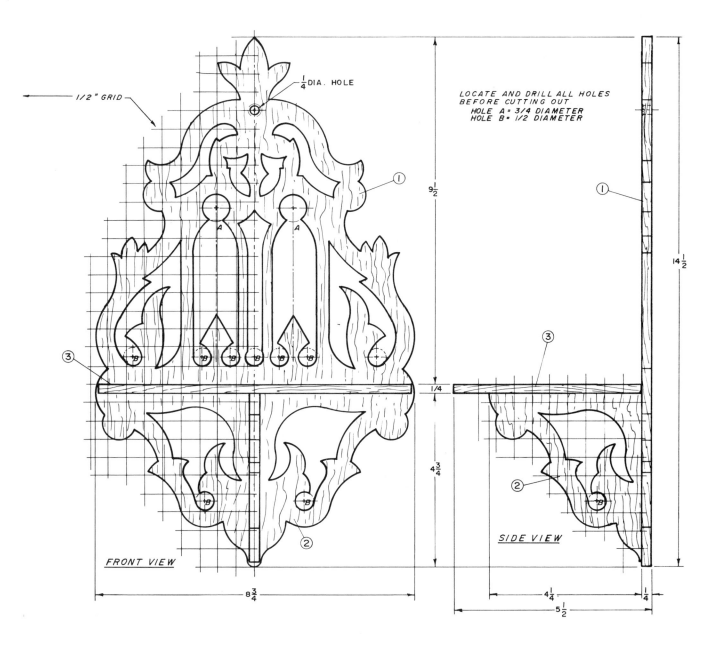

The brace pattern is nothing more than one half the bottom, left side of the backboard. To get the shape, simply trace the cutout backboard onto a piece of wood, and then cut it out. Make a simple pattern of the shelf, and cut it out. The paper pattern can be easily sanded off, if you used the rubber cement. Resand all parts before assembly. Drill small holes for all brads before nailing so that the wood will not split.

Finishing

Glue and tack all the parts together as shown in the exploded view. Check that everything is square. Apply two coats of a clear, satin finish, such as varnish, shellac, or deft (laquer). Your shelf is ready to be put up, and it will be enjoyed for years and years to come.

24 ♦ Wall Mirror, circa 1930

This is another interesting project, especially for those with scroll saws—or very ambitious individuals with a hand coping saw. It is a takeoff of a popular mirror design from the 1930s. With a parallel-arm scroll saw it takes about two hours to make all the intricate interior cuts. There are over forty interior cuts, so it helps if your scroll saw blade can be removed and reattached in about 30 seconds. I recommend a straight-grained hardwood such as walnut.

Instructions

Cut all of the wood to size per the cutting list. Sand the face board using fine grit sandpaper.

On a piece of tracing paper (or vellum) that is about ten inches by sixteen inches, draw a vertical midline. To the left of the midline draw a 1/2-inch grid. Carefully transfer the design to the grid, point by point. Locate the two 1/2-inch diameter holes. Fold the paper along the midline, and retrace the pattern on the right-hand side. This will ensure an exact pattern for both sides.

Glue the paper pattern to the wood using rubber cement or a spray-mount adhesive. Carefully locate and drill the four 1/2-inch diameter holes. Also drill with care a 1/8-inch diameter hole in the middle of each of the forty or so inner openings for inserting the blade to make the interior cuts. Take care not to rip through the back while drilling the holes. Resand the bottom surface to remove all burrs made by drilling the holes. You want to have a smooth back surface while sawing so the blade will not hang up any place.

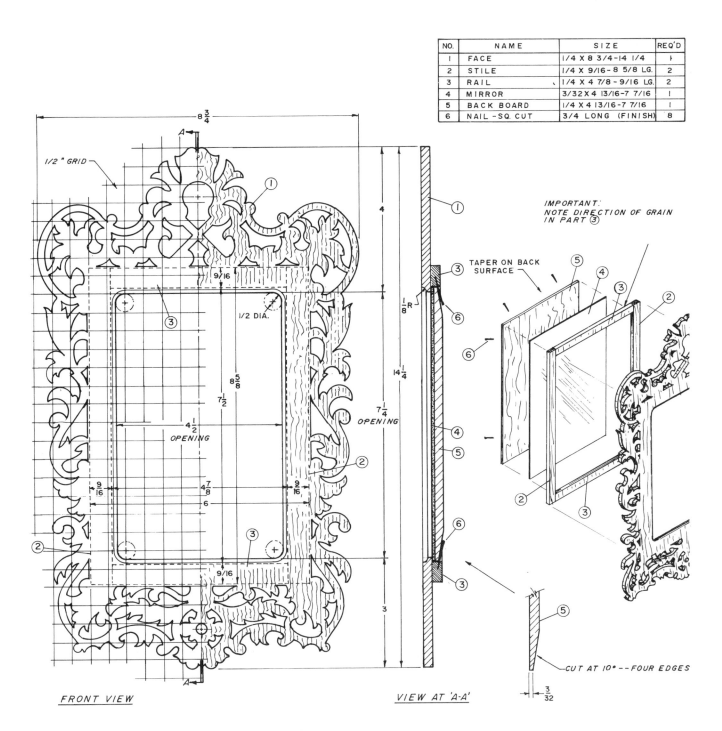

NO.	NAME	SIZE	REQ'D
1	FACE	1/4 X 8 3/4-14 1/4	1
2	STILE	1/4 X 9/16- 8 5/8 LG.	2
3	RAIL	1/4 X 4 7/8 - 9/16 LG.	2
4	MIRROR	3/32 X 4 13/16-7 7/16	1
5	BACK BOARD	1/4 X 4 13/16-7 7/16	1
6	NAIL -SQ. CUT	3/4 LONG (FINISH)	8

1/2 " GRID

IMPORTANT:
NOTE DIRECTION OF GRAIN
IN PART ③

TAPER ON BACK
SURFACE

CUT AT 10° -- FOUR EDGES

FRONT VIEW

VIEW AT 'A-A'

Carefully make all interior cuts. If you go off the lines a little, try to do the same thing on the opposite side so that both sides will be the same. Lightly resand the back surface again to remove any burrs. Cut the outer edge with care. Remove the paper pattern and resand the top and bottom surfaces.

Using a router with a ball-bearing follower, make a 1/8-inch radius cove cut around the inside 4 1/2-inch by 7 1/2-inch opening. On the back surface, glue the stiles and rails in place. Note the direction of grain in the rails; it is important that the grain run in this direction so the mirror will not warp.

Purchase a mirror slightly smaller than the opening within the stile and rail assembly, and cut a backboard about the same size. Note: the back edge of the backboard is cut at a 10 degree angle leaving about a 3/32-inch edge on all four sides. See detail of backboard.

75

25 ◆ Dutch Maid Whirligig

Perhaps after the weather vane, the whirligig represents true American Folk Art. Whirligigs depicted most every human endeavor. This is a takeoff of a whirligig that was sold at an antique auction nearby a couple of years ago. It was in a very "weathered" condition and brought several hundred dollars. That seemed high to me as I didn't think it was actually "antique," yet. I judged it was made in the early thirties or so, at most about 60 years old rather than the 100 or more years old usually needed to be called an antique. The purchasers were happy, so that's all that really matters. Nevertheless, it was an interesting whirligig, so I took a photograph and made a few measurements of its overall dimensions.

Here is my version of the "antique" Dutch Maid Whirligig. Be sure to make everything "loose-jointed," since you cannot afford any "drag" anyplace or the wind will not turn the very small blades. I suggest purchasing all of the brass parts *before* starting so that you can fit each part as you make the project. Note that you will need a temporary stand. Make this temporary stand before starting the whirligig proper, so that you can support the assembly as you put it together and test it. Any piece of wood for the stand will do.

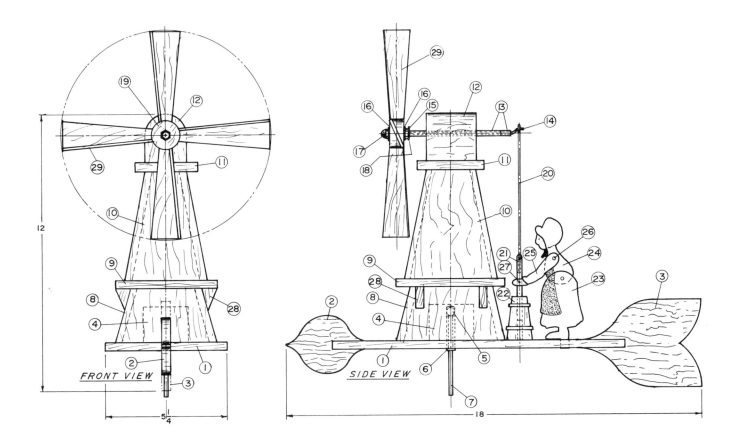

FRONT VIEW

SIDE VIEW

Instructions

Study how the project is assembled and how it works. Cut all parts to size per the cutting list. Locate and drill all holes as you make each piece. Carefully lay out and cut each part, especially taking care to lay out the base correctly. The locations of the 1/4-inch diameter hole, the bucket, and the two 1/4-inch by 1/2-inch slots are important also for the project to assemble correctly.

Glue together the four base walls and the four upper walls. After the glue sets, sand the top and bottom surfaces so they are perfectly flat. Locate and glue the support block to the base. Drill a 1/4-inch diameter hole up from the bottom of the base and into the support block about 1 1/2-inches deep. Insert the pivot bearing (round steel ball) and pivot tube into the hole. It should be a tight fit so that the bearing and tube will not fall out. Glue the rest of the windmill house together as shown in the exploded view. Attach the four side braces. The bucket will need to be turned on a lathe. Attach the bucket to the base as indicated. Slide the brass shaft tube into the cap section. This also should be a tight fit.

Temporarily put the Dutch maid together with the special post-and-head screws. Make sure the pieces move freely without any hang-ups. Temporarily add the handle to the bucket and to the maid's hands. Use a simple pin made of soft wire; bend the ends to keep it in place.

Temporarily add the assembled fan blade with the nut, washers, and acorn lock nut. Add the piston wire. Note: drill a tight-fitting hole in the tip of the bucket handle, as shown. Slowly turn the fan blade to check that everything functions smoothly, and adjust if necessary.

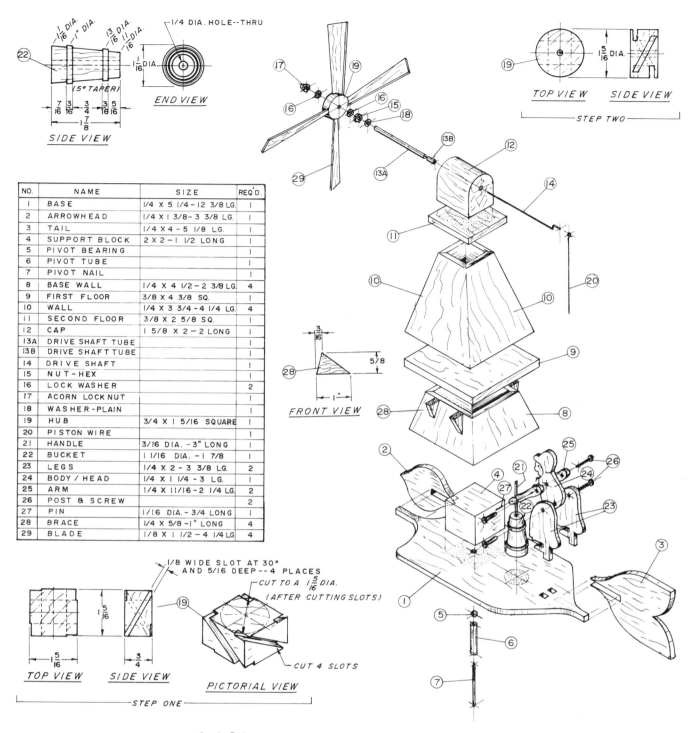

NO.	NAME	SIZE	REQ'D.
1	BASE	1/4 X 5 1/4 - 12 3/8 LG.	1
2	ARROWHEAD	1/4 X 1 3/8 - 3 3/8 LG.	1
3	TAIL	1/4 X 4 - 5 1/8 LG.	1
4	SUPPORT BLOCK	2 X 2 - 1 1/2 LONG	1
5	PIVOT BEARING		1
6	PIVOT TUBE		1
7	PIVOT NAIL		1
8	BASE WALL	1/4 X 4 1/2 - 2 3/8 LG.	4
9	FIRST FLOOR	3/8 X 4 3/8 SQ.	1
10	WALL	1/4 X 3 3/4 - 4 1/4 LG.	4
11	SECOND FLOOR	3/8 X 2 5/8 SQ.	1
12	CAP	1 5/8 X 2 - 2 LONG	1
13A	DRIVE SHAFT TUBE		1
13B	DRIVE SHAFT TUBE		1
14	DRIVE SHAFT		1
15	NUT - HEX		1
16	LOCK WASHER		2
17	ACORN LOCK NUT		1
18	WASHER - PLAIN		1
19	HUB	3/4 X 1 5/16 SQUARE	1
20	PISTON WIRE		1
21	HANDLE	3/16 DIA. - 3" LONG	1
22	BUCKET	1 1/16 DIA. - 1 7/8	1
23	LEGS	1/4 X 2 - 3 3/8 LG.	2
24	BODY / HEAD	1/4 X 1 1/4 - 3 LG.	1
25	ARM	1/4 X 11/16 - 2 1/4 LG.	2
26	POST & SCREW		2
27	PIN	1/16 DIA. - 3/4 LONG	1
28	BRACE	1/4 X 5/8 - 1" LONG	4
29	BLADE	1/8 X 1 1/2 - 4 1/4 LG	4

Finishing

Disassemble the Dutch maid, piston wire, and fan assembly. Prime the entire project with exterior primer. Paint your windmill to suit, using bright colors and your imagination. This is the particularly fun part of the project. You can add a little, or as much, detail as you wish. Try not to get layers of paint so thick that they restrict any movement.

Apply a coat of paste wax to all of the pieces. Reassemble the fan, piston wire, and Dutch maid. Recheck that everything functions smoothly with little effort. Don't forget that this whirligig has such small blades that any friction must be minimized. Mount your whirligig on a post, and watch the Dutch maid churn butter.

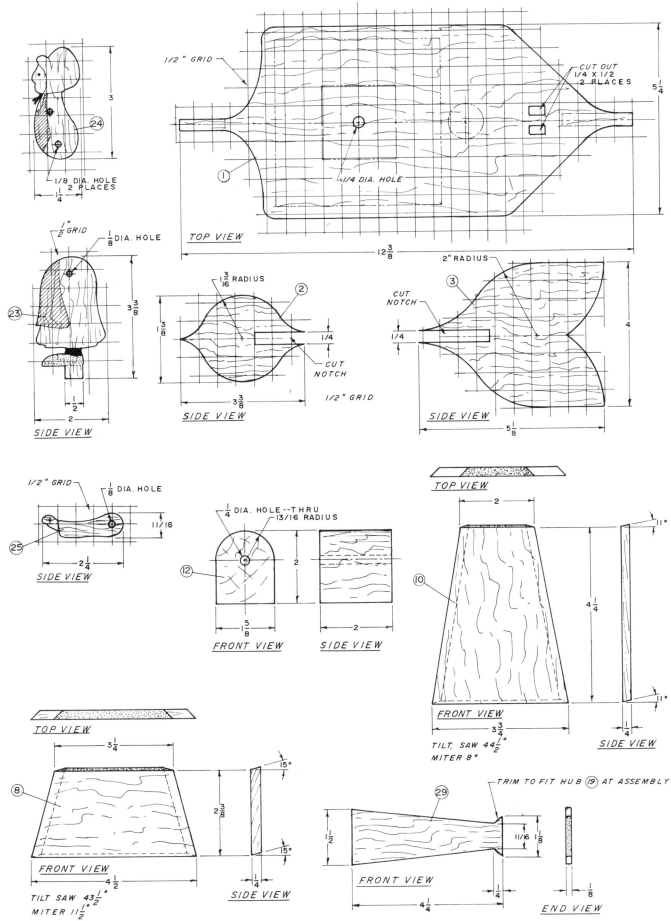

1/8 DIA. HOLE
1/4   2 PLACES

24

3

1/2" GRID

CUT OUT
1/4 X 1/2
2 PLACES

5 1/4

TOP VIEW

1/4 DIA. HOLE

1

12 3/8

1/2" GRID

1/8 DIA. HOLE

23

3 3/8

1/2

2

SIDE VIEW

1 3/16 RADIUS

2

1 3/8

1/4

CUT
NOTCH

3 3/8

1/2" GRID

SIDE VIEW

2" RADIUS

3

CUT
NOTCH

1/4

4

SIDE VIEW

5 1/8

TOP VIEW

1/2" GRID

1/8 DIA. HOLE

25

11/16

2 1/4

SIDE VIEW

1/4 DIA. HOLE--THRU
13/16 RADIUS

12

2

1 5/8

FRONT VIEW

2

2

SIDE VIEW

2

10

4 1/4

11°

11°

3 3/4

1/4

SIDE VIEW

TILT. SAW 44 1/2°
MITER 8°

TOP VIEW

3 1/4

8

2 3/8

15°

15°

4 1/2

1/4

SIDE VIEW

TILT SAW 43 1/2°
MITER 11 1/2°

FRONT VIEW

TRIM TO FIT HUB 19 AT ASSEMBLY

29

1 1/2

11/16 1 1/8

4 1/4

1/4

FRONT VIEW

1/8

END VIEW

79

TOY AND PUZZLE PROJECTS

26 ◆ Dinosaur Puzzle

Young children's puzzles such as this one are popular today. They are easy to make, do not take much time, and can be made with most any scrap wood you have around. This puzzle was designed for a scroll saw with an 18-inch throat. If you have a smaller scroll saw, lay out a 3/8-inch grid instead of the 1/2-inch grid. This will make your puzzle about 15-inches wide rather than the 20 inches as drawn. I would suggest 1/4-inch to 3/8-inch thick plywood. I also glued a 1/8-inch thick piece of plywood *behind* the 3/8-inch plywood to provide a backing to support the pieces for the puzzle shown in the photo. This is optional.

Instructions

Cut the 1/4-inch or 3/8-inch thick piece of plywood to a size of about 14 inches by 20 inches. As plywood *can* be somewhat rough, at least on one side, fill and sand all over. Before starting, try to get a nice smooth surface on the top and bottom. Paint the back surface some neutral color such as white or yellow. Lay out the pattern on the grid and transfer the shape to the wood. Cut out the outer oval shape and sand the edges. Drill a 1/16-inch diameter hole at the mouth as shown on the plans. Insert the blade and carefully cut the outer puzzle surface free from the oval. With the dinosaur removed from the oval, make the cuts for the pieces. It really does not matter *which* pieces are cut first. Try to cut all pieces exactly as shown, but if you are off a little, no one will ever know.

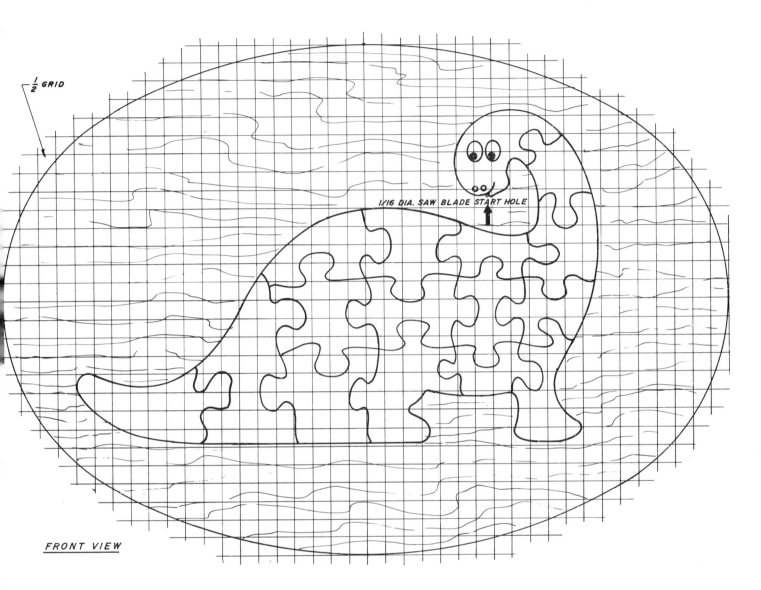

½ GRID

1/16 DIA. SAW BLADE START HOLE

FRONT VIEW

Finishing

Remove the dinosaur and paint the oval a nice bright color, such as red or blue. Paint the *top* surface of the body a gray or greenish gray. Use a nontoxic paint. Try *not* to get any paint on the edges of the pieces. I shaded the outer edge of the body a little to give it "depth" and to aid the children in putting the puzzle together.

Apply a coat of paste wax. Reassemble the puzzle and it is ready to be enjoyed.

27♦Antique Walking Penguin Toy

Here is a toy that walks, yet it has no batteries or motors. It is a copy of a now antique toy enjoyed by children in an earlier time. Years ago, "walking" toys came in all kinds of shapes and sizes—even four-legged animals. I found this one in an antiques shop in St. Johnsbury, Vermont. One foot was missing, but once repaired it walks just fine. To make it walk, you need only a smooth, slightly inclined surface.

Before you plan to get started, note that you will need a lathe to make this toy.

Instructions

Turn the body in a lathe exactly as shown. Be sure to hollow out the interior. Locate and drill the 1/16-inch diameter hole, 7/16 of an inch down from the top as shown. Carefully make the 1/16-inch wide saw kerf for the tail at a 45 degree angle as shown.

Turn the head on a lathe. Check that the 7/8-inch diameter "neck" fits tightly into the body. Drill a 1/4-inch diameter hole 1/2-inch deep at 10 degrees as shown for the beak. Make up a beak and glue it to the head.

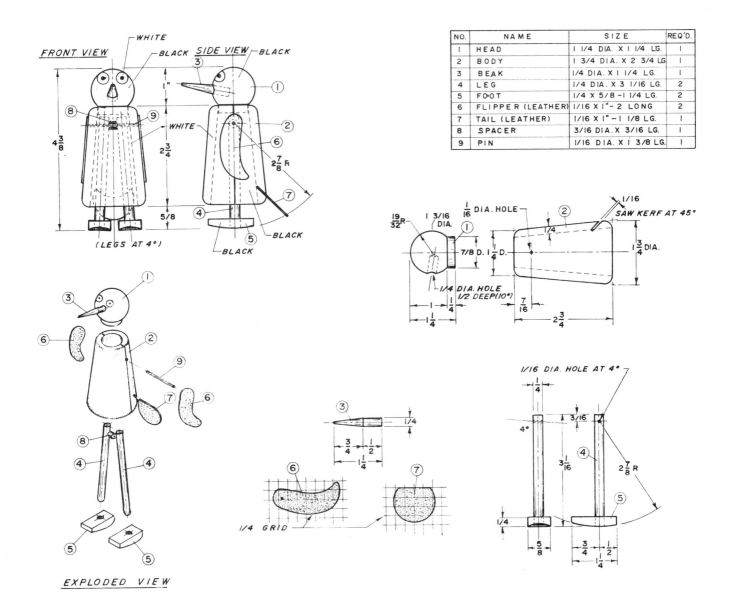

NO.	NAME	SIZE	REQ'D.
1	HEAD	1 1/4 DIA. X 1 1/4 LG.	1
2	BODY	1 3/4 DIA. X 2 3/4 LG.	1
3	BEAK	1/4 DIA. X 1 1/4 LG.	1
4	LEG	1/4 DIA. X 3 1/16 LG.	2
5	FOOT	1/4 X 5/8 - 1 1/4 LG.	2
6	FLIPPER (LEATHER)	1/16 X 1" - 2 LONG	2
7	TAIL (LEATHER)	1/16 X 1" - 1 1/8 LG.	1
8	SPACER	3/16 DIA. X 3/16 LG.	1
9	PIN	1/16 DIA. X 1 3/8 LG.	1

Cut the two legs from 1/4-inch diameter dowel, and carefully locate and drill a 1/16-inch diameter hole at 4 degrees as shown. Make up the feet and glue them to the legs. Important: be sure they are 90 degrees to the 1/16-inch diameter hole. Check the 2 7/8-inch radius from the hole to the bottom of the feet—this is crucial for the toy to "walk." Assemble the legs and feet to the body with 1/16-inch diameter stiff wire and a small spacer piece between legs; a small piece of tubing or a large bead will do. There should be a tight fit between the wire and body, but a loose fit between the wire and legs; the legs must swing freely.

Finishing

Paint the body, head, and legs white and black, to suit, using a nontoxic paint. Carefully cut the wings and tail from a piece of 1/16-inch thick black leather or plastic (leather was used on the original). Attach the wings and tail, and your penguin is ready to walk. Place it at the top of a smooth, slightly inclined surface and watch him walk. You have turned back time to the turn of the last century.

28 ◆ Two-Piece Toy Roadster, circa 1930

On a summer's day, I was browsing at a local antiques shop when I found this peculiar small, toy car. While it is probably not an actual antique, it is rather old; I estimate about 60 years old since it depicts an early 1930s roadster, perhaps a Cadillac. What fascinated me the most about this unique find was that the body was made of only *two* simple pieces. They were interlocked in such a way that they created a full-bodied car. I purchased it and drew up the plans just as the original toy was. The roadster is easy to make, does not take much time, and would make an excellent gift for any child. The child will have fun and get a sense of what another child may have played with in the earlier part of the 1900s.

Note: this project is more properly termed *folk art* rather than the reproduction of an antique. Therefore, the painted finish does *not* have to be perfect. It should *look* handmade; so if you are *not* an expert painter—as I surely am *not*—don't be afraid to do this project. You can always buy a *perfect* plastic toy at any toy store.

Instructions

Step 1. Cut two pieces of knot-free, softwood such as pine; one, 3/4-inch thick by 2 1/8-inch wide and 6 1/4 inches long; and another 3/4-inch thick by 1 3/4-inch wide and 7 inches long. Sand the top and bottom surfaces.

Step 2. Transfer the shapes of the body and base to the wood, and cut the 3/4-inch wide, 1/2-inch deep notch in the base piece. Check that the body fits snugly into the notch in the base.

Step 3. Cut the body and base to shape according to the drawing, and sand all edges. Take care to line up the wheelwells for the two pieces.

Step 4. Glue these two pieces together and the major part of the roadster is complete. Fill, if necessary, with wood filler, and resand all over.

Step 5. Cut the wheels and spare tires from a one-inch diameter dowel—two pieces 1 1/2-inches long, and two pieces 1/4-inch long.

Step 6. Glue them in place as shown.

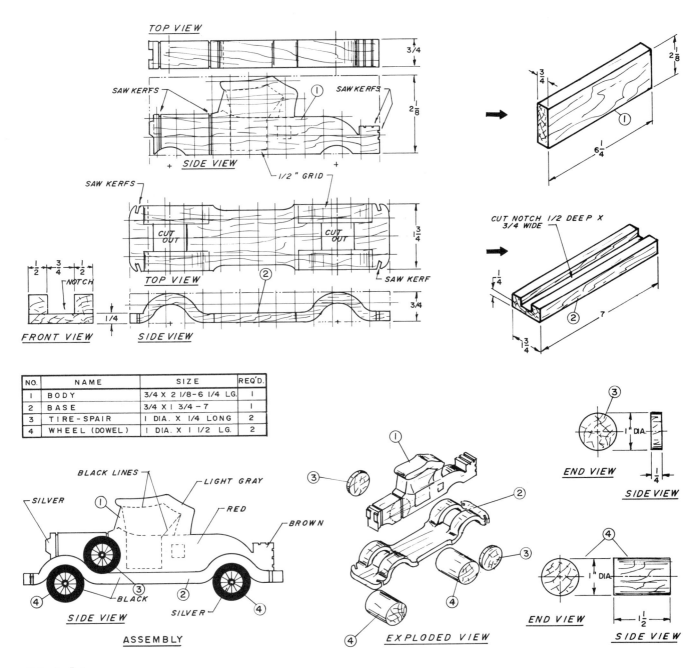

NO.	NAME	SIZE	REQ'D.
1	BODY	3/4 X 2 1/8-6 1/4 LG.	1
2	BASE	3/4 X 1 3/4 - 7	1
3	TIRE-SPAIR	1 DIA. X 1/4 LONG	2
4	WHEEL (DOWEL)	1 DIA. X 1 1/2 LG.	2

Finishing

Step 7. Prime all over, and lightly sand when dry.

Step 8. Paint the roadster as you desire—the original colors are noted if you wish to follow them.

Step 9. (optional) If you want your car to *look* 60 years old, you might want to carefully sand some of the edges down to the bare wood where you think it might have been worn naturally in normal use. Apply a glaze coat of dark walnut stain over the entire painted car—even over the white paint. This will give it an authentic old look and feel.

Your car is now ready to be enjoyed for another 60 years. As this might become a family "heirloom," you might want to cut your name and date into the bottom of the car. Perhaps in the middle of the twenty-first century some woodworker will find *your* car in an antiques shop and be as fascinated with *it* as I was with the original I found.

29 ◆ Toy Soldier Puzzle

Here is a simple puzzle for children two to six years of age. "Simple," yet actually it is a three-dimensional puzzle. It makes a great project for you and, brightly painted, will provide hours of fun for a child or grandchild, yours or a friend's. You will need a lathe for this project.

Instructions

Turn the body to size and drill a 1 1/16-inch diameter hole in one end, 2 1/4 inches deep. At the other end, drill a 9/16-inch diameter hole, 1 1/4 inches deep. Carefully locate and drill a 1/4-inch diameter hole through from the side, 7/16 of an inch deep. Sand all over.

Turn the base, hat, head, collar, and two arms, as shown. Just be sure all parts fit loosely—not tightly the way you usually want. Sand all parts all over.

Glue the arm support to the body and glue the leg to the base; all other parts are loose.

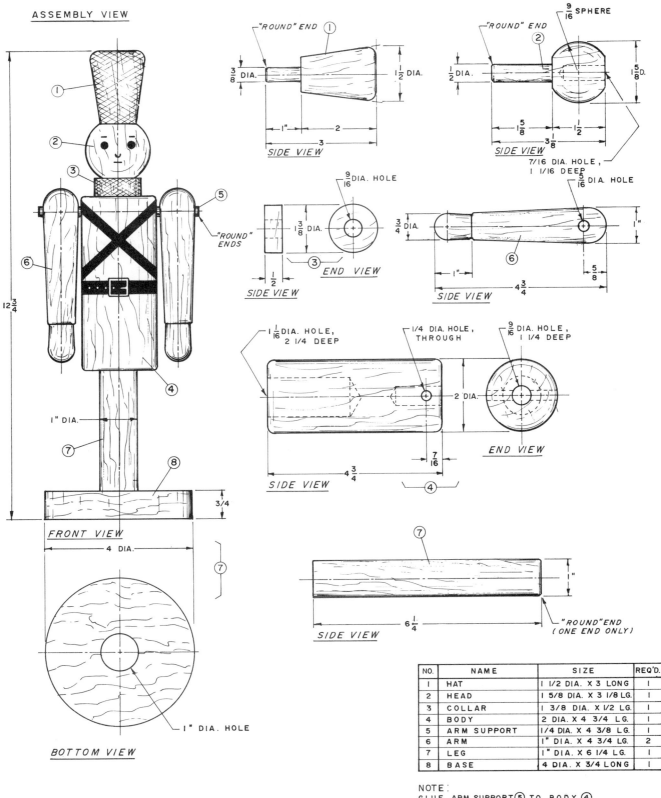

ASSEMBLY VIEW

$\frac{9}{16}$ SPHERE

"ROUND" END ①

"ROUND" END

$\frac{3}{8}$ DIA.

$1\frac{1}{2}$ DIA.

$\frac{1}{2}$ DIA.

$1\frac{5}{8}$ D.

1" 2

3

SIDE VIEW

$1\frac{5}{8}$ $1\frac{1}{2}$

$3\frac{1}{8}$

SIDE VIEW

7/16 DIA. HOLE,
1 1/16 DEEP

$\frac{9}{16}$ DIA. HOLE

$\frac{5}{16}$ DIA. HOLE

$1\frac{3}{8}$ DIA.

$\frac{3}{4}$ DIA.

1"

$\frac{1}{2}$

③ END VIEW

SIDE VIEW

1"

$4\frac{3}{4}$

$\frac{5}{8}$

SIDE VIEW

$12\frac{3}{4}$

"ROUND"
ENDS

1 $\frac{1}{16}$ DIA. HOLE,
2 1/4 DEEP

1/4 DIA. HOLE,
THROUGH

$\frac{9}{16}$ DIA. HOLE,
1 1/4 DEEP

2 DIA.

END VIEW

$4\frac{3}{4}$

$\frac{7}{16}$

SIDE VIEW

④

1" DIA.

⑦

FRONT VIEW

4 DIA.

⑦

1"

SIDE VIEW

$6\frac{1}{4}$

"ROUND" END
(ONE END ONLY)

$\frac{3}{4}$

1" DIA. HOLE

BOTTOM VIEW

NO.	NAME	SIZE	REQ'D.
1	HAT	1 1/2 DIA. X 3 LONG	1
2	HEAD	1 5/8 DIA. X 3 1/8 LG.	1
3	COLLAR	1 3/8 DIA. X 1/2 LG.	1
4	BODY	2 DIA. X 4 3/4 LG.	1
5	ARM SUPPORT	1/4 DIA. X 4 3/8 LG.	1
6	ARM	1" DIA. X 4 3/4 LG.	2
7	LEG	1" DIA. X 6 1/4 LG.	1
8	BASE	4 DIA. X 3/4 LONG	1

NOTE:
GLUE ARM SUPPORT ⑤ TO BODY ④
GLUE LEG ⑦ TO BASE ⑧

Finishing

Paint your soldier with bright, nontoxic paints. Use your imagination when doing the details and add whatever you think a soldier would look like. Now, how does this puzzle go together? Change "two to six years of age" to "children of all ages!"

30♦Rabbit Pull Toy

All children enjoy a pull toy at some time or another. My two-year-old granddaughter, Hilary, enjoys pull toys. I don't know how much longer she will enjoy them, but she certainly likes them at this age.

Instructions

Make the base and drill four, 5/16-inch diameter holes for the axle pegs. If you have a dowel-centering jig, use it to ensure that the holes are properly positioned. If the holes are *not* centered, the pull toy will rock. Drill a 1/16-inch diameter hole at 45 degrees in the front for the pull string or use a small eyescrew as I did as shown in the photo. Locate and drill two 1/4-inch diameter holes for the dowel pins. Sand all over. Round all edges slightly to eliminate any sharp corners.

Lay out the rabbit design on a 1/2-inch grid—transfer the pattern to the wood and cut it out. Drill a 5/16-inch diameter hole for the eyes. Sand all edges slightly as necessary.

Glue the rabbit in place. When the glue sets, drill up through the two 1/4-inch diameter holes in the base into the rabbit's legs and glue the two dowel pins in place. This will give the rabbit added strength.

Finishing

Use only nontoxic paint. Paint the rabbit and base. Paint the wheels and hub of the axle pegs. When the paint dries, glue the axle pegs in place. Be sure *not* to get any glue on the wheels. Add the pull string and "pull."

Now off to see if your rabbit can "catch" your child, grandchild, or some other lucky youngster you had in mind!

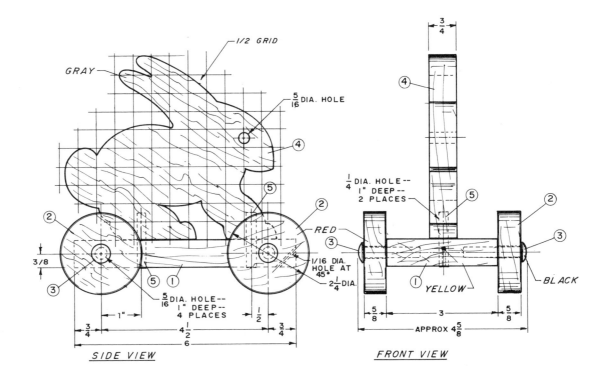

1/2 GRID

GRAY

5/16 DIA. HOLE

④

⑤

②

⑤

①

3/8

③

5/16 DIA. HOLE --
1" DEEP --
4 PLACES

3/4

1"

4 1/2

6

1/2

3/4

SIDE VIEW

3/4

④

1/4 DIA. HOLE --
1" DEEP --
2 PLACES

⑤

②

RED

③

①   YELLOW

1/16 DIA.
HOLE AT
45°

2 1/4 DIA.

③

BLACK

5/8

3

5/8

APPROX 4 5/8

FRONT VIEW

NO	NAME	SIZE	REQ'D.
1	BASE	3/4 X 3 - 6 LONG	1
2	WHEEL (2 1/4 DIA.)		4
3	AXLE PEG		4
4	BODY	3/4 X 5 - 6 LONG	1
5	DOWEL PIN	1/4 DIA. X 1 1/2 LG.	2
6	PULL	3/4 DIA. X 3 LONG	1
7	TWINE	TO SUIT	1

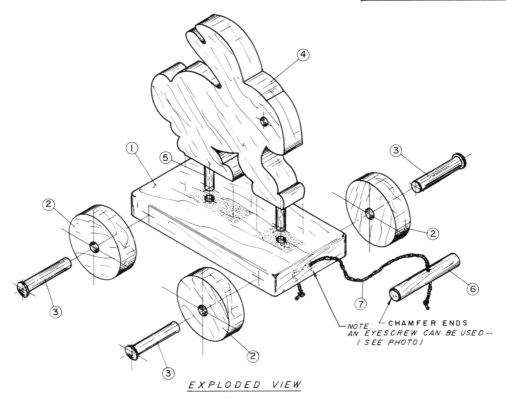

④

③

①

⑤

②

③

②

②

③

⑦

⑥

③

②

③

NOTE:
AN EYESCREW CAN BE USED --
(SEE PHOTO)

CHAMFER ENDS

EXPLODED VIEW

31◆Farm Tractor

Here is a heavy-duty farm tractor any child would love to have. A sense of freedom, fresh air, power. Having spent many hours on a big green tractor on a farm in northern Vermont, I know the real thrill of owning and operating a tractor. Now you can give some special youngster the same thrill.

If you have a scroll saw, this project is very easy to make. I recommend that you use hardwood, especially for the fenders.

Instructions

Lay out the body design on a 1/4-inch grid, point by point. Transfer the pattern to the wood and cut it out. Locate and drill all of the holes. Sand all over.

Make a few saw kerfs along the front to simulate a grill. Trim the drawbar as shown in the exploded view. Don't forget to add the air filter to the left side. Cut the fenders from one piece of wood, 3/4-inch by 1 1/8-inch and 1 3/4 inches long, as shown. The wheels are simply cut from dowels, 1 1/2-inch diameter and 2-inch diameter. The two front spacers are cut from a 5/8-inch diameter dowel. Assemble the parts, referring to the exploded view.

Finishing

Paint with a nontoxic paint. Most tractors in North America are painted red, blue, or green. Paint the wheels black or to suit. The tractor is now ready for some heavy farm work in the hands of an imaginative child.

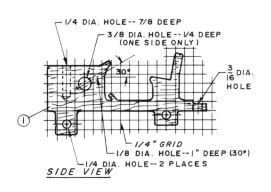

1/4 DIA. HOLE-- 7/8 DEEP

3/8 DIA. HOLE-- 1/4 DEEP
(ONE SIDE ONLY)

30°

3/16 DIA. HOLE

1/4" GRID

1/8 DIA. HOLE--1" DEEP (30°)

1/4 DIA. HOLE--2 PLACES

SIDE VIEW

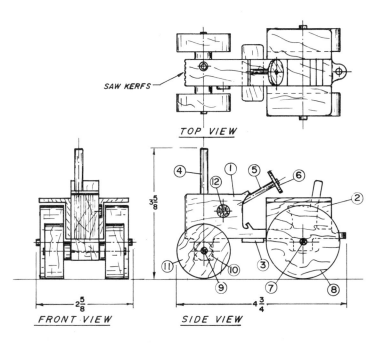

SAW KERFS

TOP VIEW

3 5/8

2 5/8

FRONT VIEW

4 3/4

SIDE VIEW

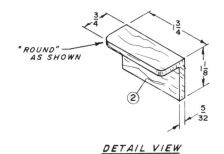

3/4

1 3/4

"ROUND" AS SHOWN

1 1/8

5/32

DETAIL VIEW

NO.	NAME	SIZE	REQ'D.
1	BODY	3/4 X 2 1/4 - 4 1/2 LG.	1
2	FENDER	3/4 X 1 1/8 - 1 3/4 LG.	2
3	STEP	1/8 X 5/8 - 1 1/2 LG.	1
4	STACK	1/4 DIA.-2 LONG	1
5	COLUMN	1/8 DIA.- 2 LONG	1
6	WHEEL	3/4 DIA.-1/8 LONG	1
7	REAR AXLE	1/4 DIA.-2 3/4 LG.	1
8	REAR WHEEL	2 DIA.-3/4 LONG	2
9	FRONT AXLE	1/4 DIA.-2 1/4 LG.	1
10	SPACER	5/8 DIA.-1/4 LONG	2
11	FRONT WHEEL	1 1/2 DIA.-1/2 LONG	2
12	AIR CLEANER	3/8 DIA. X 3/8 LG.	1

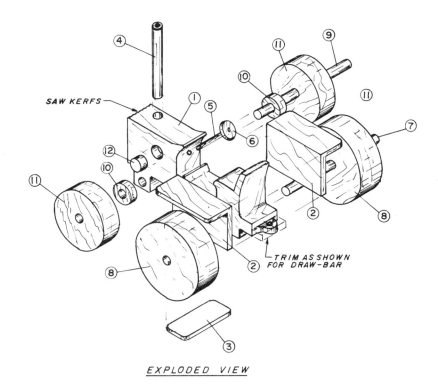

SAW KERFS

TRIM AS SHOWN FOR DRAW-BAR

EXPLODED VIEW

91

32 ♦ Off-Road Vehicle

Here is a toy that surely all children will want to get their hands on. These days, real off-road vehicles are very popular; some can be equipped as fancy as a high-priced car—with all kinds of extras including air conditioning! If you have a scroll saw with a 2-inch cutting depth, this project will be very simple to make.

Instructions

The body assembly is made of three simple pieces; 2-inch thick center body with two matching 3/16-inch thick side panels. The wheels can be purchased from a supply house or simply cut from 1 1/4-inch dowel.

Lay out and transfer the shape of the body and two sides to the wood. (I taped the two sides together when I cut out mine so that they would be identical.) On the body, carefully locate and drill the nine 1/4-inch diameter holes. Locate and drill the one 7/16-inch diameter hole. Cut out the body.

Locate the 1/8-inch diameter hole for the steering wheel column. Drill it at about 40 degrees, as shown. Attach the column and steering wheel. Read the section below on finishing before you glue the two side panels to the center body section. After the sides and center have been glued and the glue has set, carefully trim or sand all edges so the body edges all line up and are smooth. Cut or sand the front hood taper, as shown, starting about 1 1/2-inch from the front of the body.

Cut and fit the front and rear fenders as shown. Notice that the two front fenders must be cut to fit the taper of the body. Glue the fenders in place. Using a sharp chisel, make the notches for the two headlights. Add the front and rear bumpers. Add the spare tire if you would like to have one. You will have to drill a 1/4-inch diameter hole through the back of the body. Cut an extra axle peg shorter for holding the spare tire in place.

Add the wheels and axle pegs; check that everything turns freely. For added realism, you may want to locate and drill eight, 1/8-inch diameter holes around the wheels as shown. This completes the assembly.

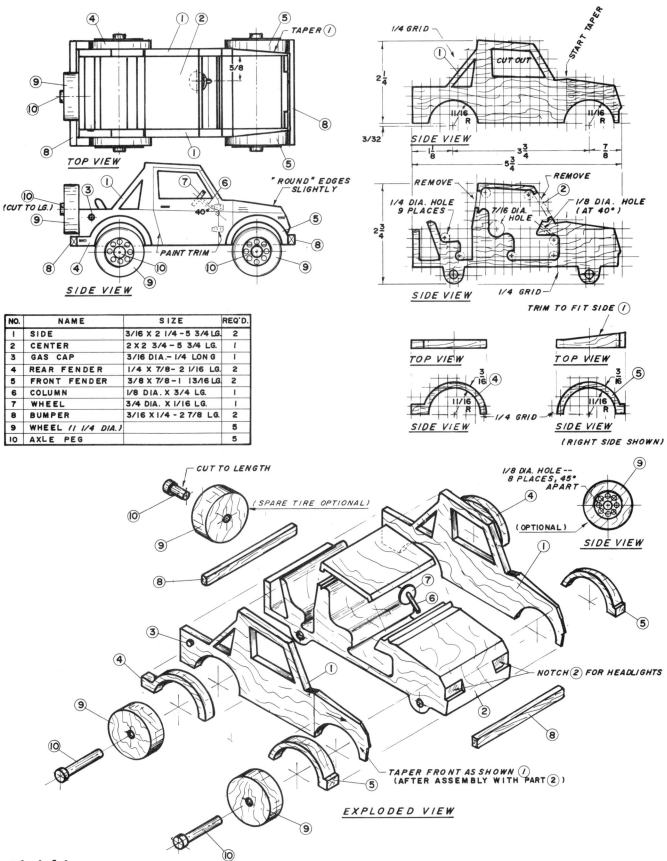

NO.	NAME	SIZE	REQ'D.
I	SIDE	3/16 X 2 1/4 – 5 3/4 LG.	2
2	CENTER	2 X 2 3/4 – 5 3/4 LG.	1
3	GAS CAP	3/16 DIA.– 1/4 LONG	1
4	REAR FENDER	1/4 X 7/8 – 2 1/16 LG.	2
5	FRONT FENDER	3/8 X 7/8 – 1 13/16 LG.	2
6	COLUMN	1/8 DIA. X 3/4 LG.	1
7	WHEEL	3/4 DIA. X 1/16 LG.	1
8	BUMPER	3/16 X 1/4 – 2 7/8 LG.	2
9	WHEEL (1 1/4 DIA.)		5
10	AXLE PEG		5

TOP VIEW

SIDE VIEW

"ROUND" EDGES SLIGHTLY

PAINT TRIM

TAPER ①

SIDE VIEW

SIDE VIEW

TOP VIEW

TOP VIEW

SIDE VIEW

SIDE VIEW

(RIGHT SIDE SHOWN)

TRIM TO FIT SIDE ①

EXPLODED VIEW

CUT TO LENGTH

(SPARE TIRE OPTIONAL)

NOTCH ② FOR HEADLIGHTS

TAPER FRONT AS SHOWN ①
(AFTER ASSEMBLY WITH PART ②)

1/8 DIA. HOLE --
8 PLACES, 45°
APART

(OPTIONAL)

SIDE VIEW

Finishing

The toy can be left natural with only a wax finish or it can be painted. If
you paint your vehicle, be sure to use only nontoxic paint.

93

33 ◆ Wagoneer Van

This project is made exactly like the off-road vehicle, project number 32. It is made up of a body, two sides, and two fender trim pieces. Study the exploded view and you can see just how simple the project is to make. If you have a scroll saw, this project will be a snap!

Instructions

Carefully lay out the parts full size, and transfer the patterns to the wood. Locate and drill all the 1/4-inch diameter holes before making any cuts. This will ensure that all the curves are exactly the same size and shape.

Cut all of the parts out. Locate and drill a 3/16-inch diameter hole for the steering wheel at 22 degrees, as shown. Add the column and steering wheel to the body.

Glue the sides to the body, and trim or sand as necessary. Fit and glue the fender mouldings to the sides, and trim or sand as necessary. Add the wheels and axle pegs. Be sure the wheels turn freely. Note: the wheels can be cut from 1 1/2-inch diameter dowel and held in place with 1/4-inch diameter dowel. You might want to add the wheels after painting.

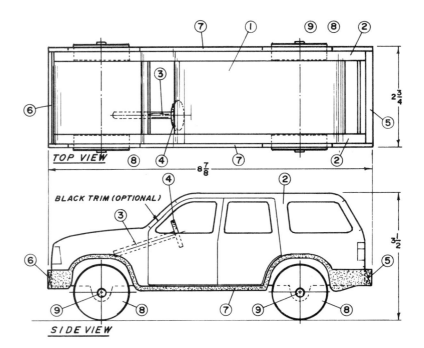

TOP VIEW

⑧ ④ ⑦ ②

8⅞

BLACK TRIM (OPTIONAL)

SIDE VIEW

2¾

3½

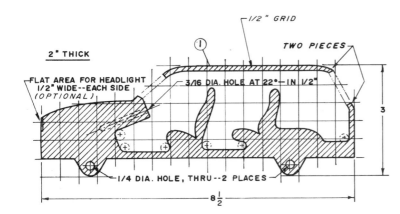

2" THICK

½" GRID

TWO PIECES

FLAT AREA FOR HEADLIGHT
½" WIDE--EACH SIDE
(OPTIONAL)

3/16 DIA. HOLE AT 22°-- IN ½"

¼ DIA. HOLE, THRU--2 PLACES

8½

3

NO.	NAME	SIZE	REQ'D.
1	BODY	2 X 3 - 8 1/8 LONG	1
2	SIDE PANEL	1/4 X 2 11/16 - 8 1/2 LG.	2
3	COLUMN	3/16 .DIA. X 1 3/4 LG.	1
4	STEERING WHEEL	3/4 DIA. X 1/8 LG.	1
5	REAR BUMPER	1/4 X 7/16 - 2 1/2 LG.	1
6	FRONT BUMPER	1/8 X 1/2 - 2 1/2 LG.	1
7	TRIM	1/8 X 1" - 9 LONG	2
8	WHEEL (1 1/2 DIA.)		4
9	AXLE PEG		4

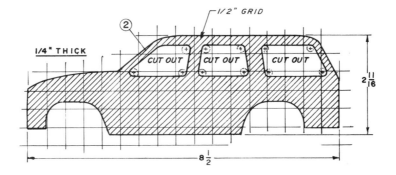

½" GRID

1/4" THICK

CUT OUT   CUT OUT   CUT OUT

2 11/16

8½

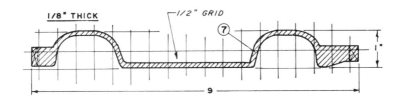

1/8" THICK

½" GRID

⑦

1"

9

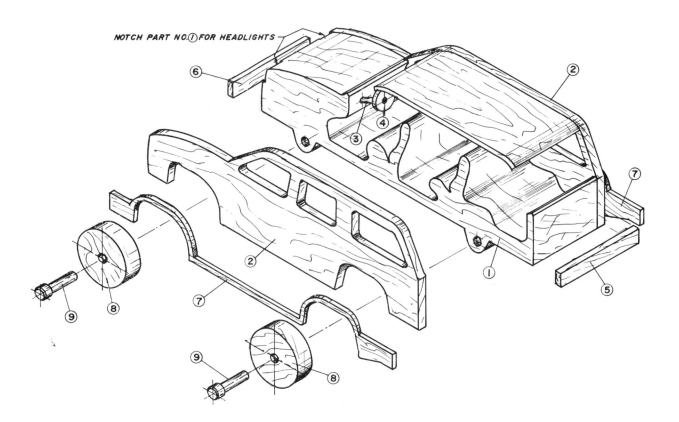

NOTCH PART NO. ① FOR HEADLIGHTS

EXPLODED VIEW

Finishing

Paint your toy wagoneer to suit with a nontoxic paint. Your wagoneer is
ready to roll!

34 ♦ Walking Dog Pull Toy

Now this is *my* kind of dog. You don't have to feed, walk, or brush him. He doesn't bark or smell—*and* you don't have to apply flea powder to him. This dog's legs move as you pull it, making it look like a real dog walking. This kind of dog used to be a common addition to many kids' toy chests maybe thirty or so years ago.

Instructions

Carefully lay out all of the parts on a 1/2-inch grid, point by point. Don't forget to locate all of the drilling points for the holes. I suggest that you simply glue two 3/4-inch thick pieces together to get the 1 1/2-inch thickness for the body.

Transfer the patterns to the wood. Locate and drill all of the holes first, before you cut out all of the pieces. After cutting them out, sand all over. Multiple parts that are the same should be drilled, cut out, and sanded along the edges while they are taped or tacked together to ensure that each matches exactly.

Dry-fit all of the parts to ensure that everything works correctly. Adjust as necessary. Make sure that all of the parts are a little on the loose side so that the dog will pull easily and the four legs will move smoothly without any binding.

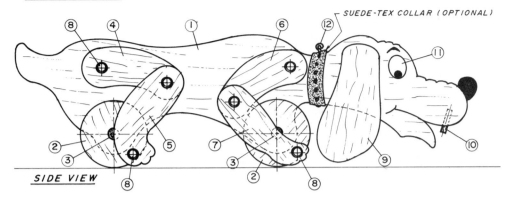

SUEDE-TEX COLLAR (OPTIONAL)

SIDE VIEW

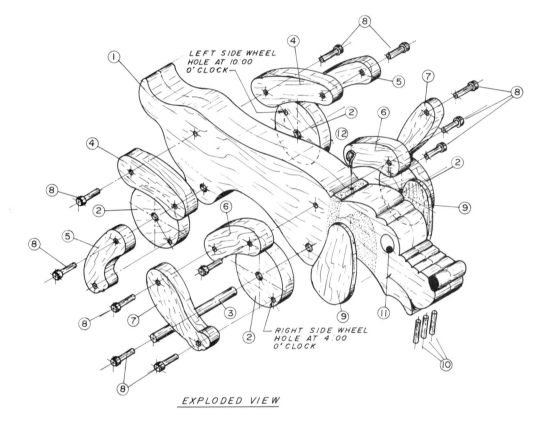

LEFT SIDE WHEEL
HOLE AT 10:00
O'CLOCK

RIGHT SIDE WHEEL
HOLE AT 4:00
O'CLOCK

EXPLODED VIEW

Finishing

Disassemble and paint your walking dog as you wish. If you have always wanted a "spotted" dog, here is your chance to have one. Don't forget the collar. Apply a coat of paste wax to all of the parts before final assembly, but do not get any wax inside any hole where you will be gluing an axle peg.

Carefully glue the axle pegs in place with the wheels on the peg. Be sure the glue does *not* get on the wheels. Check that all parts move freely. Add an eyescrew to the "collar" and get our your leash; it's time to walk the dog.

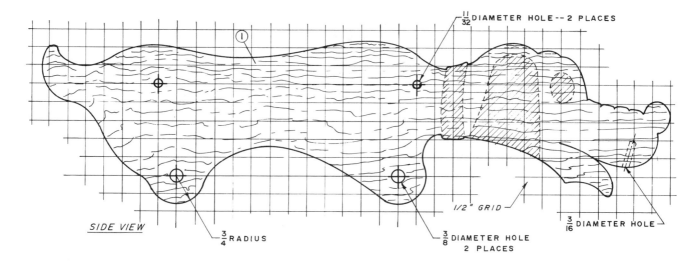

①

$\frac{11}{32}$ DIAMETER HOLE -- 2 PLACES

1/2" GRID

$\frac{3}{16}$ DIAMETER HOLE

$\frac{3}{4}$ RADIUS

$\frac{3}{8}$ DIAMETER HOLE
2 PLACES

SIDE VIEW

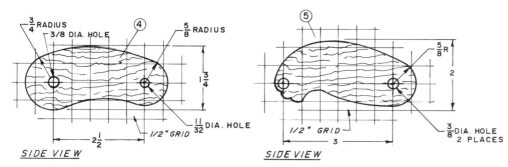

$\frac{3}{4}$ RADIUS
3/8 DIA. HOLE

④

$\frac{5}{8}$ RADIUS

$1\frac{3}{4}$

$2\frac{1}{2}$

1/2" GRID

$\frac{11}{32}$ DIA. HOLE

SIDE VIEW

⑤

$\frac{5}{8}$ R

2

1/2" GRID

$\frac{3}{8}$ DIA. HOLE
2 PLACES

3

SIDE VIEW

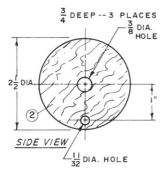

$\frac{3}{4}$ DEEP -- 3 PLACES

$\frac{3}{8}$ DIA. HOLE

$2\frac{1}{2}$ DIA.

1"

②

SIDE VIEW

$\frac{11}{32}$ DIA. HOLE

NO.	NAME	SIZE	REQ'D.
1	BODY	1 1/2 X 4 1/2 -17 1/2	1
2	WHEEL	3/4 X 2 1/2 DIAMETER	4
3	AXLE	3/8 DIA. X 3 1/16 LG.	2
4	BACK LEG - TOP	3/4 X 1 3/4 - 4 LG.	2
5	BACK LEG - BOTTOM	5/8 X 2 - 4 LONG	2
6	FRONT LEG - TOP	3/4 X 1 5/8 - 3 3/4 LG.	2
7	FRONT LEG - BOTTOM	5/8 X 1 9/16 - 4 LG.	2
✱ 8	AXLE PEG		12
9	E A R	5/16 X 2 1/4 - 4 1/2	2
10	TEETH	3/16 DIA. X 1 1/8 LG.	3
11	EYE - JIGGLE		2
12	SCREW EYE		1

✱ CUT OFF TO 1 3/8 " LONG

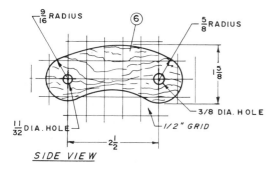

$\frac{9}{16}$ RADIUS

⑥

$\frac{5}{8}$ RADIUS

$1\frac{5}{8}$

$\frac{11}{32}$ DIA. HOLE

3/8 DIA. HOLE

1/2" GRID

$2\frac{1}{2}$

SIDE VIEW

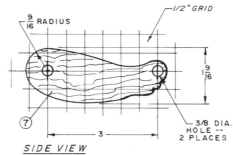

$\frac{9}{16}$ RADIUS

1/2" GRID

$1\frac{9}{16}$

⑦

3

3/8 DIA.
HOLE --
2 PLACES

SIDE VIEW

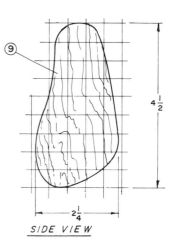

⑨

$4\frac{1}{2}$

$2\frac{1}{4}$

SIDE VIEW

35 ♦ Carousel with Sixteen Horses

The carousel tournament or game was "discovered" during the medieval Crusades in Asia Minor. In the 12th century Arab and Turkish horsemen played a game called "Little War." This was played with the riders moving their horses in a circle as clay balls filled with scented water were tossed in. The object of the game was not to miss a catch. The game was brought to France by about the time Columbus was setting sail from Spain to happen upon the West Indies and America.

Around 1680, mechanical horses were suspended by chains from arms radiating from a center pole and rotated. A horse, mule, or man supplied the motive power. This marks the development of the first carousel, or merry-go-round, as we recognize it. Trying to grab the brass ring was added to the ride. Some years later, the English added steam power to the carousel.

In 1850, the first United States patent for a carousel was granted to Eliphalet S. Scripture of Green Point, (Brooklyn) New York, patent number 7419. His invention gave the horses a galloping up-and-down motion by using an integrated suspension system.

Horses were beautifully carved by skilled craftsmen and were brightly painted. These hand-carved horses are true Folk Art. Elaborate trimmings and facades were added to the carousel. Horses on actual carousels typically have a "romantic" side and a plain side. The side that is seen from outside the carousel is the romantic—very fancy—side.

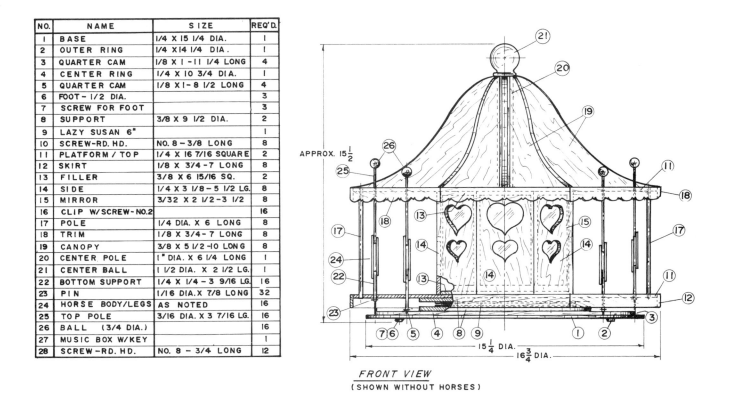

NO.	NAME	SIZE	REQ'D.
1	BASE	1/4 X 15 1/4 DIA.	1
2	OUTER RING	1/4 X 14 1/4 DIA.	1
3	QUARTER CAM	1/8 X 1 –11 1/4 LONG	4
4	CENTER RING	1/4 X 10 3/4 DIA.	1
5	QUARTER CAM	1/8 X 1–8 1/2 LONG	4
6	FOOT – 1/2 DIA.		3
7	SCREW FOR FOOT		3
8	SUPPORT	3/8 X 9 1/2 DIA.	2
9	LAZY SUSAN 6"		1
10	SCREW–RD. HD.	NO. 8 – 3/8 LONG	8
11	PLATFORM / TOP	1/4 X 16 7/16 SQUARE	2
12	SKIRT	1/8 X 3/4 –7 LONG	8
13	FILLER	3/8 X 6 15/16 SQ.	2
14	SIDE	1/4 X 3 1/8 – 5 1/2 LG.	8
15	MIRROR	3/32 X 2 1/2 –3 1/2	8
16	CLIP W/ SCREW– NO.2		16
17	POLE	1/4 DIA. X 6 LONG	8
18	TRIM	1/8 X 3/4 –7 LONG	8
19	CANOPY	3/8 X 5 1/2 –10 LONG	8
20	CENTER POLE	1" DIA. X 6 1/4 LONG	1
21	CENTER BALL	1 1/2 DIA. X 2 1/2 LG.	1
22	BOTTOM SUPPORT	1/4 X 1/4 – 3 9/16 LG.	16
23	PIN	1/16 DIA. X 7/8 LONG	32
24	HORSE BODY/LEGS	AS NOTED	16
25	TOP POLE	3/16 DIA. X 3 7/16 LG.	16
26	BALL (3/4 DIA.)		16
27	MUSIC BOX W/KEY		1
28	SCREW –RD. HD.	NO. 8 – 3/4 LONG	12

APPROX. 15 1/2

15 1/4 DIA.

16 3/4 DIA.

FRONT VIEW
(SHOWN WITHOUT HORSES)

From 1890 to 1920 some of the most beautiful carousels were built. Exciting music from a band organ—often mistakingly called a calliope—made the carousel ride even more exciting. The band organ had measured rhythm provided by the crash of cymbals and beating drums. In later years the mighty Wurlitzer concert band organ was made and added to many carousels.

Of the thousands of carousels built throughout the world, fewer than one hundred remain in existence. Through the years, fire has destroyed most of them. In the United States over 2500 were in operation by 1900, it is estimated. Today only 52 are left. Those that are left are now quite valuable.

Instructions

Carefully study the exploded view before starting anything. Be sure you fully understand how the carousel works before you get going. The sixteen horses go up and down as the platform rotates above two harmonic cams running around in concentric circles beneath the poles for the horses. On the whole, this is very simple, but accuracy in all layouts is a must if everything is to work together correctly.

The sixteen 1/4-inch square holes in the base *must* be located exactly as shown around the center. The sixteen 3/16-inch diameter holes must also be located exactly as shown around the center *and* in line with the square holes. The two cams must also be located exactly around the same center.

Cut all of the pieces of the carousel at first only to size as shown. Assemble the base, outer ring, center ring, and cams as shown. Be sure everything is around an exact center point. Position the lazy Susan on the two supports temporarily, using 1/2-inch diameter dowel about eight inches long as a guide. Glue the bottom support to the base assembly.

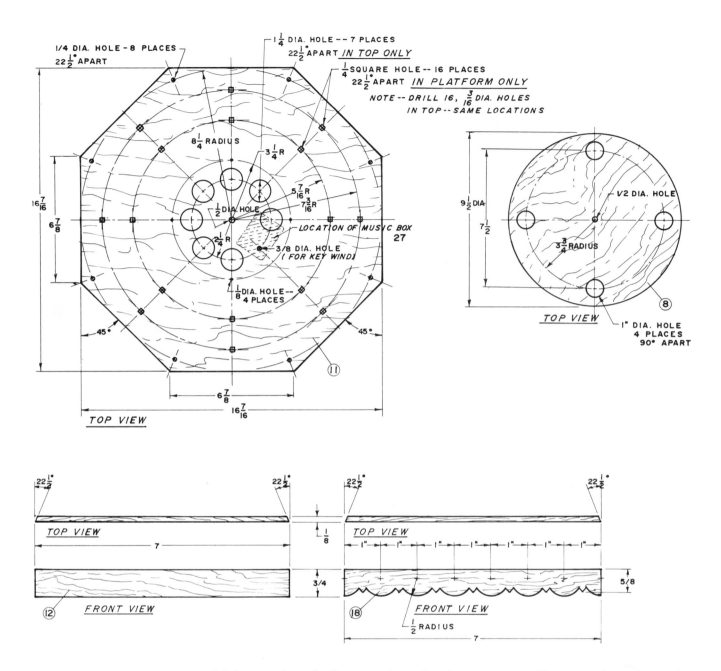

1/4 DIA. HOLE - 8 PLACES
22 1/2° APART

1 1/4 DIA. HOLE -- 7 PLACES
22 1/2° APART *IN TOP ONLY*

1/4 SQUARE HOLE -- 16 PLACES
22 1/2° APART *IN PLATFORM ONLY*

NOTE -- DRILL 16, 3/16 DIA. HOLES
IN TOP -- SAME LOCATIONS

8 1/4 RADIUS

3 1/4 R

5 7/16 R

7 3/16 R

1/2 DIA. HOLE

LOCATION OF MUSIC BOX
27

2 1/4 R

3/8 DIA. HOLE
(FOR KEY WIND)

1/8 DIA. HOLE --
4 PLACES

16 7/16

6 7/8

45°   45°

6 7/8

16 7/16

TOP VIEW

11

9 1/2 DIA.

7 1/2

1/2 DIA. HOLE

3 3/4 RADIUS

8

TOP VIEW

1" DIA. HOLE
4 PLACES
90° APART

22 1/2°   22 1/2°

TOP VIEW   1/8

7

3/4

12   *FRONT VIEW*

22 1/2°   22 1/2°

TOP VIEW   1" 1" 1" 1" 1" 1" 1"

5/8

18   *FRONT VIEW*
1/2 RADIUS
7

Make up the platform with eight skirt pieces. Glue together the eight sides and two fillers (top and bottom). Glue together the top, eight trim pieces, canopy, center pole, and center ball. Glue the center assembly to the platform, taking care to position it exactly. Temporarily screw the top and canopy assembly to the platform assembly. Be sure to add the eight poles and three rubber feet to the underside of the platform. Check that everything turns freely and works correctly.

On a piece of heavy paper, draw a 1/2-inch grid. Carefully lay out the horses' bodies and legs, as shown. Transfer the patterns for the horses' bodies to a 5/16-inch thick piece of hardwood, their legs to a 1/4-inch thick piece. Carefully cut out as closely as possible. Drill a 3/16-inch diameter hole in each body, and make a 1/4-inch wide notch *in line* with the 3/16-inch diameter holes. It is important that they *are* in line as shown. Cut out the legs. Note horses A through H are slightly larger than horses I through P. Horses A through H are outside horses. I through P are inside horses.

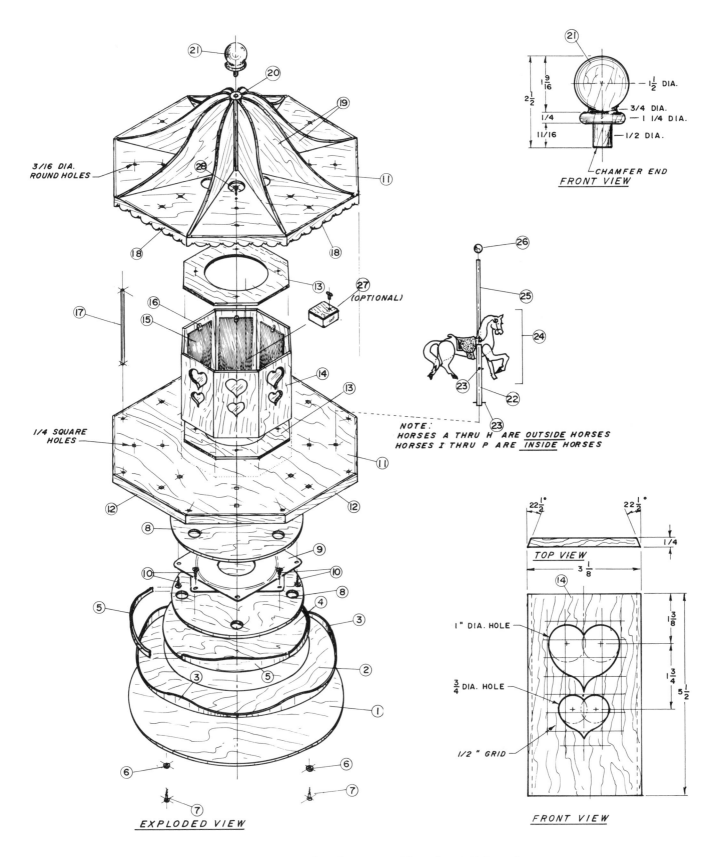

EXPLODED VIEW

3/16 DIA. ROUND HOLES

1/4 SQUARE HOLES

NOTE:
HORSES A THRU H ARE *OUTSIDE* HORSES
HORSES I THRU P ARE *INSIDE* HORSES

27 (OPTIONAL)

FRONT VIEW

21

1 9/16
2 1/2
1/4
11/16

1 1/2 DIA.
3/4 DIA.
1 1/4 DIA.
1/2 DIA.

CHAMFER END

24
25
26
23
22
23

TOP VIEW

22 1/2°   22 1/2°
3 1/8
1/4

FRONT VIEW

14

1" DIA. HOLE

3/4 DIA. HOLE

1/2" GRID

1 3/8
1 3/4
5 1/2

Glue the legs to the bodies as shown in the drawing. Glue the 3/16-inch diameter top pole and 1/4-inch square bottom support to each body, also as shown. Glue the top pin (foot rest) in place, but only drill and add the bottom pin temporarily—the bottom pin holds the horses in place so that they cannot come up through the floor.

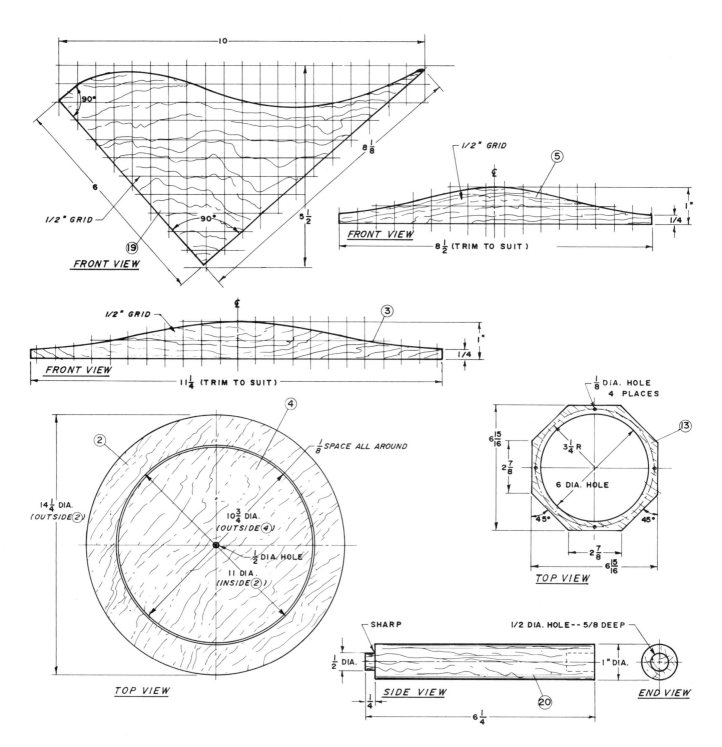

Finishing

Disassemble and paint to suit. Use your imagination; visit your local library and look up carousels to get ideas for painting yours. They were bright and of many colors. Be sure to use nontoxic paints. Sand all over. Brightly paint your horses, again referring to photographs of real carousel horses for inspiration.

Unscrew the top assembly from the carousel and add the horses; larger horses on the outside; smaller horses on the inside. Glue the bottom pins in place (under the platform). Assemble the carousel, and check that the horses go up and down without getting hung up or any binding. Make adjustments as necessary.

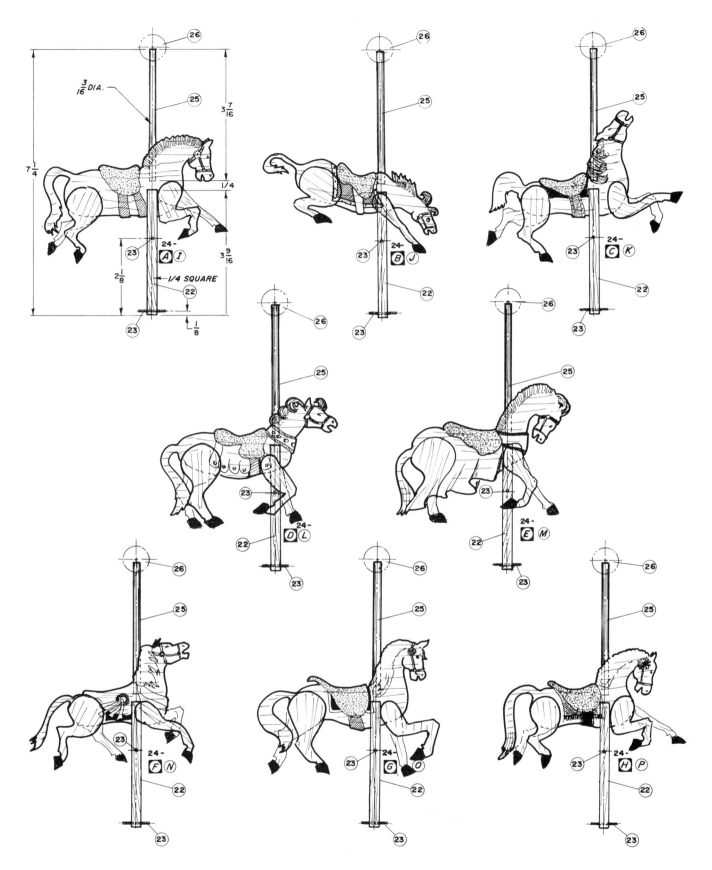

Finally, glue the 3/4-inch diameter balls on top of each pole. Now all you need is some band organ music. This is a project that should be around for many years. Be sure you sign and date it as this carousel probably will be handed down to each succeeding generation for years to come.

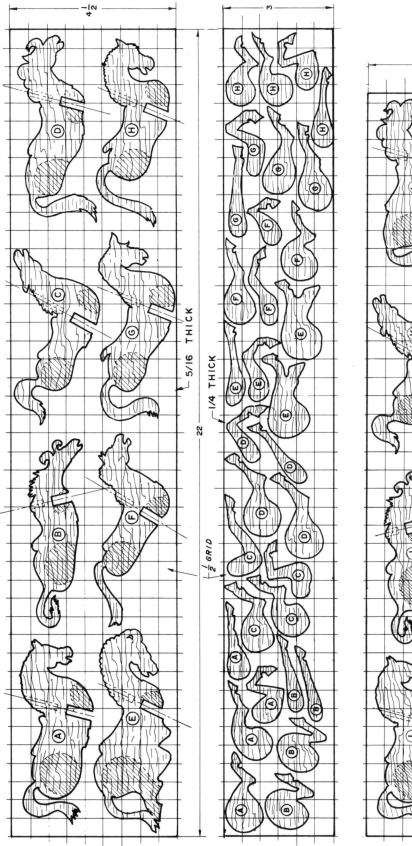

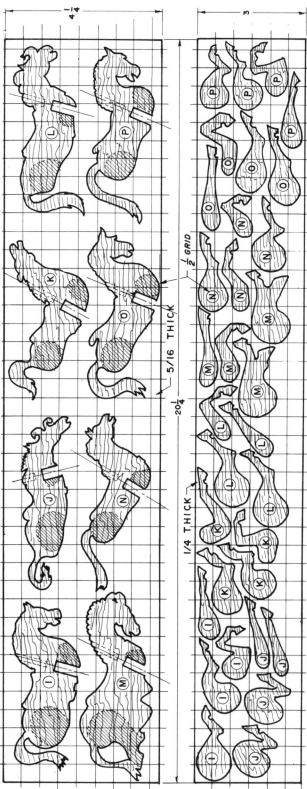

CLOCK PROJECTS

36 ◆ Child's Drummer Wall Clock

Here is a simple, inexpensive, three-piece wall clock that will brighten up any child's room.

Instructions

Carefully lay out the soldier's body pattern on 1/2-inch grid and the soldier's arm pattern on a 1/4-inch grid, as shown. Transfer the pattern to the wood and cut out the pieces. The drum can be cut out simply on a band saw and sanded or turned on a lathe. Drill or cut out a 2 5/6-inch diameter hole in the middle of the drum—there is a 2 5/16-inch (58-mm) diameter Forstner bit available. (If you plan to make several clocks using standard quartz movements, you might consider purchasing such a bit. They save a lot of time and make the job much easier.) Locate and drill the 1/8-inch diameter holes for the stick, pin, and rod. Glue the arm to the body, the stick and ball to the hand, and the rod and ball to the drum.

NO.	NAME	SIZE	REQ'D.
1	DRUM	1 X 4 1/4 DIA.	1
2	BODY	3/4 X 3 1/4 - 7 1/2	1
3	ARM	1/4 X 1 - 2 1/2 LG.	1
4	TACK	3/4 LONG	1
5	STICK	1/8 DIA. - 2 1/2 LG.	1
6	BALL	1/2 DIA.	2
7	ROD	1/8 DIA. - 1 1/2 LG.	1
8	PIN	1/8 DIA. - 1 LONG	1
9	MOVEMENT		1
10	HANGER		1

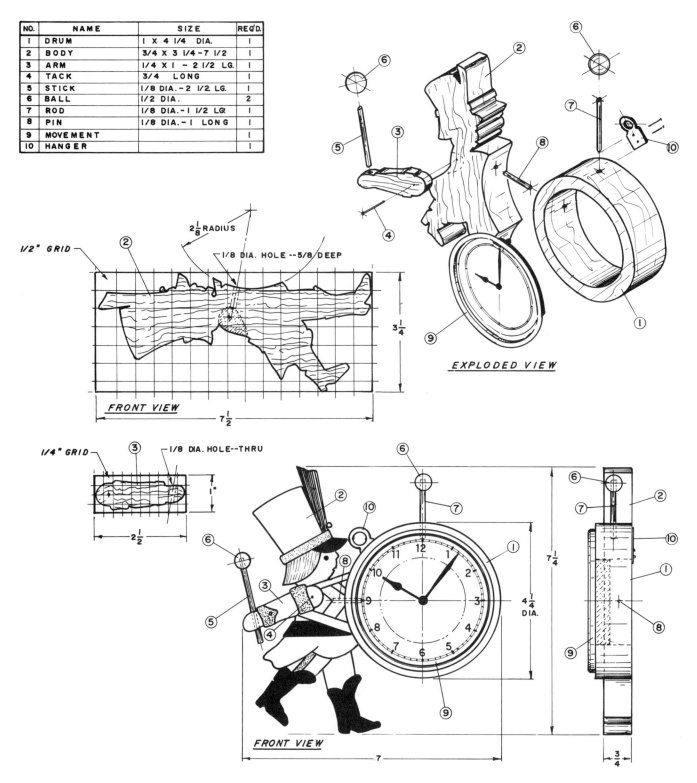

EXPLODED VIEW

2⅛ RADIUS

1/2" GRID

1/8 DIA. HOLE -- 5/8 DEEP

FRONT VIEW

3¼

7½

1/4" GRID

1/8 DIA. HOLE -- THRU

1"

2½

4¼ DIA.

7¼

3/4

FRONT VIEW

7

Finishing

Using bright colors, paint the assembled soldier and the drum to suit. Use your imagination; the design in the drawing is only a suggestion. Make your clock *your* creation. Finally, glue the drum to the soldier with the pin as a guide. Attach the hanger. Add the plastic retaining ring and insert a battery into the clock movement. Slide the clock movement into the plastic insert, and line up the twelve o'clock to the top. Your clock is now ready to teach a young child how to tell time.

37 ♦ Modern Twelve-Sided Wall Clock

This clock is simple to make. You can use scraps of wood; even the 10 3/4-inch square face can be made of glued-up scraps. Including the cost of the quartz movement and "dash" hands, this project is still very inexpensive to make. This modern-looking clock makes a great gift or an attractive item to sell at crafts fairs. A wood such as ash or oak is recommended, although most any hardwood can be used.

Instructions

Cut a starting piece for making the simple moulding for the frame, 3/4-inch by 1 1/2-inch and about 48 inches long. You might want to make up two or three starting pieces while your saw is set up to make this project even easier to build the next time—and the next. Make a 1/4-inch by 1-inch notch, as shown in the end view of the frame. Sand all surfaces, taking care to keep all of the edges sharp. Set your saw at 15 degrees and cut the twelve identical individual pieces for the frame, exactly 3 1/8-inch long, as shown.

Using masking tape, tape all twelve frame pieces together in a long line; add tape to the *outer* surfaces of all twelve pieces. Apply glue to each joint and wrap the twelve pieces into a 12-sided "circle." Apply a piece of tape at the closing joint, and let the glue set.

After the glue sets, remove the tape and sand all of the sides, back, and front surfaces.

Using the inside edge of the notch of the 12-sided frame as a template, lay out the face directly onto a piece of wood. With the frame template still on the wood for the face, mark the frame *and* face so that you can realign them into exactly the same position once the face has been cut out. Lay out the pattern as carefully as you can, since the sides will vary slightly. But, don't try for an overly tight fit; in fact, it is a good idea to let the face "float" within the frame to allow for expansion of the face. Drill a hole precisely in the middle of the face. Drill the size hole that is required by your quartz movement.

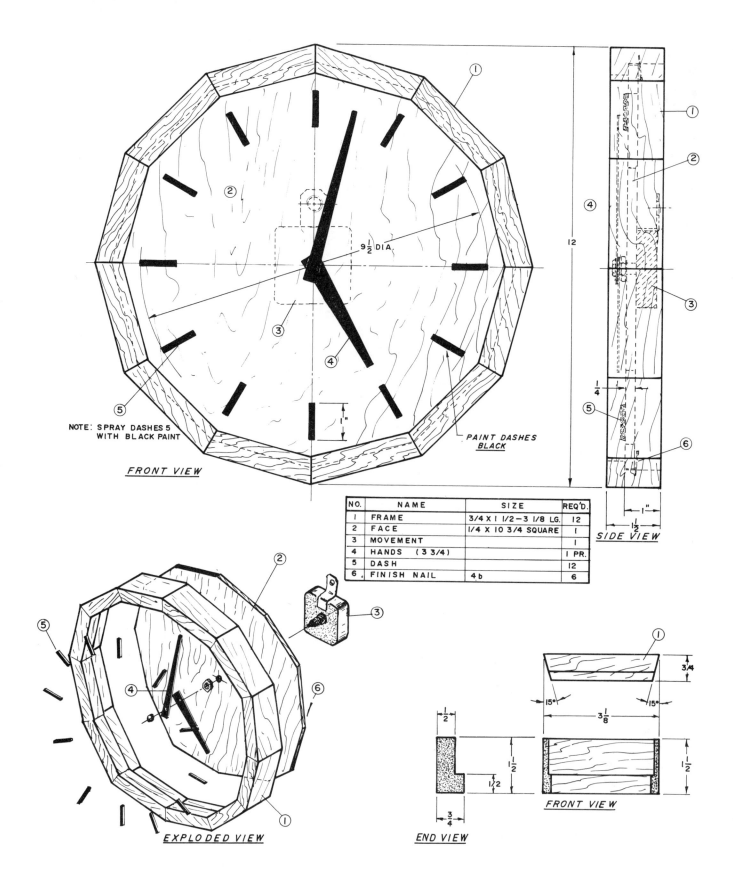

NO.	NAME	SIZE	REQ'D.
1	FRAME	3/4 X 1 1/2 – 3 1/8 LG.	12
2	FACE	1/4 X 10 3/4 SQUARE	1
3	MOVEMENT		1
4	HANDS (3 3/4)		1 PR.
5	DASH		12
6	FINISH NAIL	4 b	6

NOTE: SPRAY DASHES 5
WITH BLACK PAINT

9 1/2 DIA

PAINT DASHES
BLACK

FRONT VIEW

SIDE VIEW

EXPLODED VIEW

END VIEW

FRONT VIEW

Attach the hanger to the movement, and the movement to the clock case.
Carefully attach the hands, and install a battery. Hang it on the wall and
enjoy it! But don't forget those other frame pieces, if you made them; one
for a gift, perhaps; and one for a crafts fair.

38 ◆ Ball Wall Clock, circa 1920

Now here is an unusual design; you will either love it or hate it. I have had all kind of reactions to my ball clock. It is a takeoff of a famous design by George Nelson; I would guess from the 1920s or so. I like it because it is *so* different, so unusual. It will surely be a conversation piece anyway.

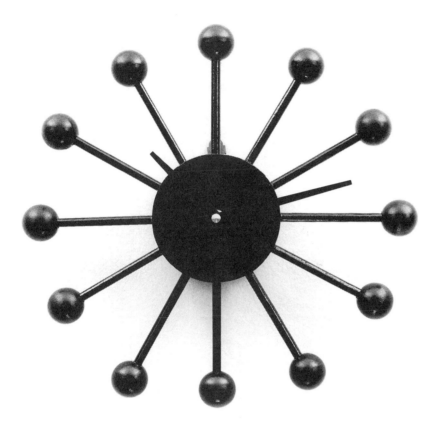

Instructions

Cut or turn the body of the clock according to the detail plans. Drill or turn the inner 3-inch diameter hole, 1 1/8-inches deep. Carefully, and as accurately as possible, lay out the twelve, 1/4-inch diameter holes equally spaced about. If you have a built-in divider on your lathe, use it to mark the center of the twelve holes. Using a "V" block on a drill press, carefully locate and drill the twelve holes. Drill a hole in the middle of the clock body for the shaft of the movement.

Glue the twelve stems in place, and then glue the twelve, one-inch spheres to the ends.

Finishing

Prime the clock body with two or three coats of primer, sanding between coats. The clock body should have a smooth, metallic-looking finish. Apply two or three coats of high-gloss paint. Black is suggested but whatever color appeals to you is fine.

Add the hanger, drilling for the screws or brads so that the clock body will not split. Add the batteries to the movement; insert the movement, and add the hands. Hang your clock on the wall and watch for people's reactions!

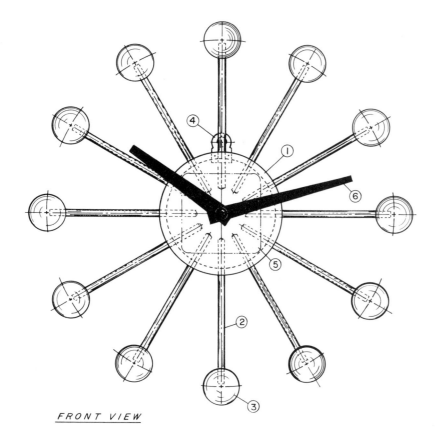

FRONT VIEW

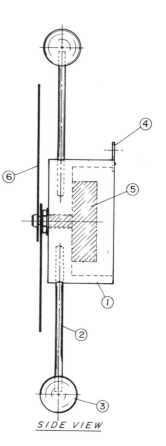

SIDE VIEW

5/16 DIA.
HOLE

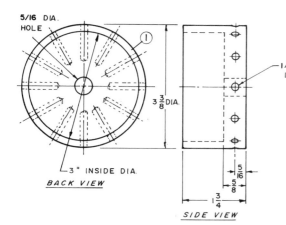

3 3/4 DIA.

3" INSIDE DIA.

BACK VIEW

SIDE VIEW

5/16

5/8

1 3/4

1/4 DIA. HOLES--1" DEEP
12 PLACES--30° APART

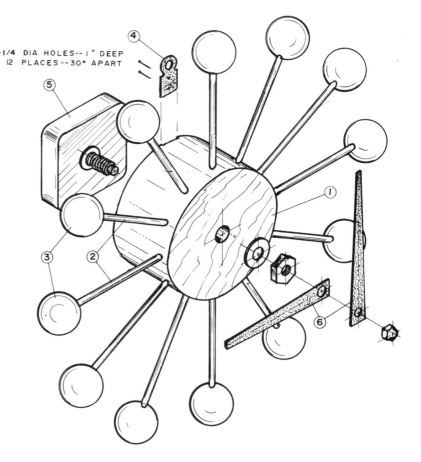

EXPLODED VIEW

NO.	NAME	SIZE	REQ'D.
I	BODY	3 3/8 DIA. - I 3/4	I
2	STEM	1/4 DIA. - 4 LG.	I2
3	BALL	I" SPHERE	I2
4	HANGERS		I
5	MOVEMENT		I
6	HANDS (3 3/4)		I PR.

39 ◆ Balloon-Style Shelf Clock

This clock design is based on an original antique clock. It is scaled down a little, but all of the proportions have been maintained for authenticity. It is actually a simple clock to make and lends a sense of formality in any room it is used in.

Instructions

Carefully, using the given dimensions, lay out the face board. Transfer the pattern to the wood, and cut it out. Sand the surfaces and sides, but keep the edges sharp. If you don't have a piece of wood for the body—1 7/8 inches by 5 1/4 inches and 8 1/8 inches long—glue up material as shown. Glue up eleven pieces—eash 3/4 inch by 1 7/8 inches by 5 1/4 inches. Using the face board as a template, draw the body shape on the glued-up wood. Carefully cut out the pattern slightly smaller than the actual face board. Glue the face board to the body, and sand the sides until smooth all around. *Keep all edges sharp.* Locate and drill a 1 5/16-inch diameter hole for the movement. A special Forstner bit can be purchased for this.

Cut the base to size, and using a 1/8-inch radius cove-cutter, cut a cove on the front and two sides as shown.

Position the base and glue it to the body and face board, taking care not to get glue on the surfaces. After the glue sets, you might want to add two flathead screws from underneath through the base to prevent the glue from coming loose, in time. This is optional and *not* shown on the plans.

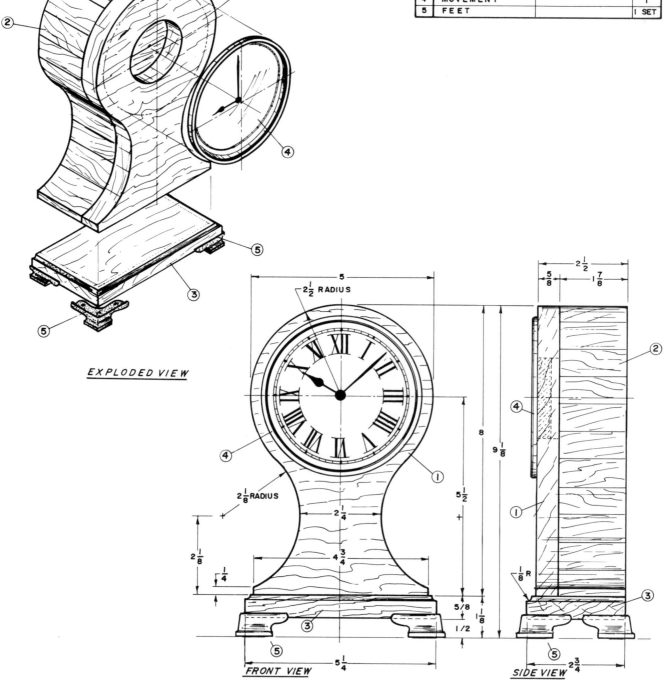

NO.	NAME	SIZE	REQ'D.
I	FACE BOARD	5/8 X 8 - 5 LONG	I
2	BODY (GLUE-UP)	3/4 X 1 7/8 - 5 1/4	II
3	BASE	5/8 X 2 3/4 - 5 1/4	I
4	MOVEMENT		I
5	FEET		I SET

EXPLODED VIEW

2½ RADIUS

2⅛ RADIUS

FRONT VIEW

SIDE VIEW

Finishing

Sand all over, stain and finish as you wish. Add the plastic retainer for the movement and the four feet. Apply a coat of paste wax. Add a battery to the movement, and insert the clock movement into the plastic retainer. Your clock is ready to be enjoyed for many years to come.

40 ♦ Galley Wall Clock

This clock acquired its name specifically because it was designed to be used in a ship's galley. This is a copy of a Waterbury galley clock, circa 1830. It was made of oak and had an eight-day brass movement. Note: the *two* hangers; this is to stop the clock from swinging back and forth in rough seas. The original movement did *not* have a pendulum—it instead had a special balance wheel escapement. Since a pendulum clock could not work on a moving, rocking ship, the balance wheel escapement had been designed to allow ships to have an accurate, dependable clock on board. This, in turn, gave early navigators—in conjunction with other instruments—the ability to calculate *exactly* where they were at all times.

You will need a lathe to make this clock.

Instructions

Study the exploded view that shows the steps involved in assembling the case. Carefully cut all of the pieces according to the plan, and glue up as shown. Be sure to use a lot of glue and to let the case assembly set for 48 hours or more before turning. You do *not* want the pieces to come apart while turning on the lathe. Position the assembly on a face plate. Take extreme care and double-check that it is in the exact center. The case will not come out right if it is not perfectly centered. Carefully turn the case while wearing a face mask and using all safety precautions. Use "VIEW AT A-A" as a guide to get the correct profile. Sand all over while the assembly is still mounted on the lathe.

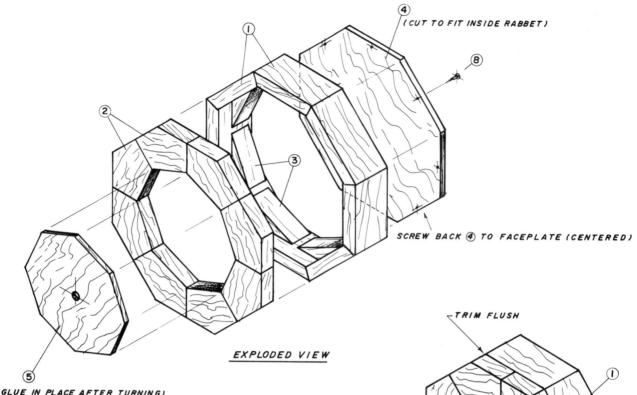

④ (CUT TO FIT INSIDE RABBET)

⑧

SCREW BACK ④ TO FACEPLATE (CENTERED)

EXPLODED VIEW

⑤

(GLUE IN PLACE <u>AFTER</u> TURNING)

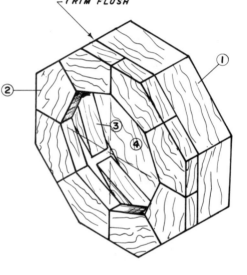

─TRIM FLUSH

AS GLUED -- READY FOR TURNING

NO.	NAME	SIZE	REQ'D.
1	SIDE	3/4 X 2 - 3 3/4 LONG	8
2	FRONT	3/4 X 2 3/16 - 3 9/16	8
3	BRACE	9/16 X 1 1/8 - 2 5/8	8
4	BACK	1/4 X 8 1/4 SQUARE	1
5	BEZEL SUPPORT	1/4 X 7 SQUARE	1
6	BEZEL 6 1/4 DIA.		1
7	MOVEMENT		1
8	SCREW-FLAT HD.	NO.6 X 5/8 LONG	8
9	HANGER - BRASS	1/2 X 1 1/8 LONG	2
10	HANDS 2 3/4 L.G.		

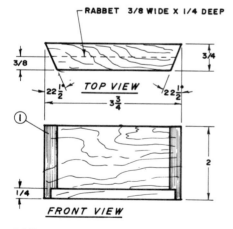

─RABBET 3/8 WIDE X 1/4 DEEP

TOP VIEW

FRONT VIEW

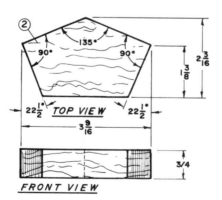

② 135° 90° 90° 22 1/2° 22 1/2°

TOP VIEW

3 9/16

FRONT VIEW

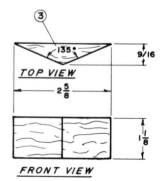

③ 135°

TOP VIEW

2 5/8

9/16

1 1/8

FRONT VIEW

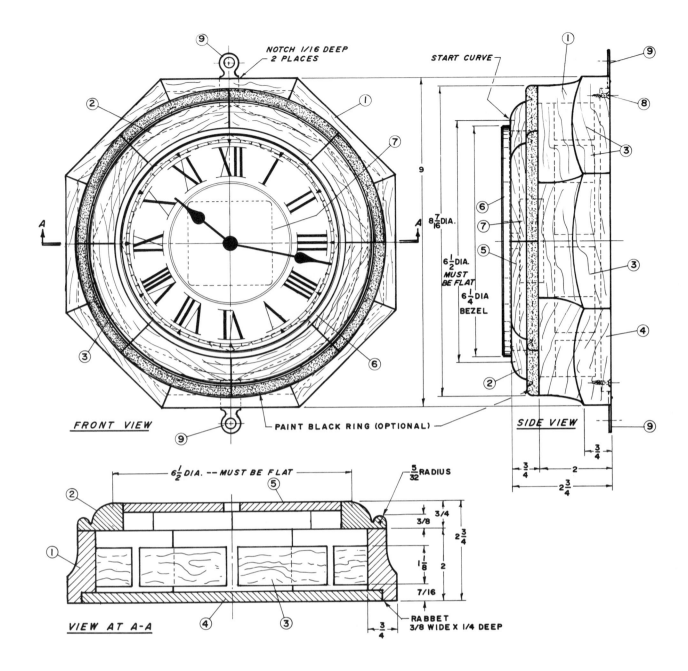

Finishing

Clean all of the surfaces and apply a stain as you desire. Apply three or four top coats of a clear finish, and lightly sand between coats. Do all of this while the case is still mounted on the lathe.

The original galley clock had a 3/8-inch wide black ring around the case as shown in the front and side views. This is optional; it is rather easy to add while the case is still mounted on the lathe. Remove the case from the face plate and drill a hole for the shaft of the movement. Add the two hangers, as shown. Mount the dial bezel to the case; add the movement and hands. All you need now is a forty-eight-foot sailboat to display your galley clock.

41 ◆ Antique Vermont Coffin Clock

This coffin clock, sometimes referred to as a box clock, is a scaled-down copy of an antique clock. The original was built by Levi Pitkin of Vermont around 1800. It was very large—over 45 inches high—had an eight-day, weight-driven movement and a hand-painted, wooden dial face. I kept the same proportions but scaled it down to 29 inches high for the smaller homes of today.

This version uses a modern quartz movement with a 20-inch long pendulum.

The case is nothing more than a box with a lid; very simple to make.

Instructions

Cut all of the parts to overall size. The case is simple box construction with 45 degree mitred corners. The back edges are rabbeted 1/4-inch wide and 1/4-inch deep for the back. The door is simply a piece of wood with two batten boards glued on at the top and bottom ends. See detail 'B' for the tounge-and-groove in the door and batten.

Assemble the case, and trim the door—with battens in place—to the size of the case. Actually it is best to fit the door so that it is *slightly larger* than the case. If the hinges are not set exactly, this will help them not show. After the door is trimmed, carefully locate and cut the two round openings— a 6 1/4-inch diameter hole, five inches down for the top opening, and a 2 1/4-inch diameter hole, 4 1/2 inches up for the bottom opening.

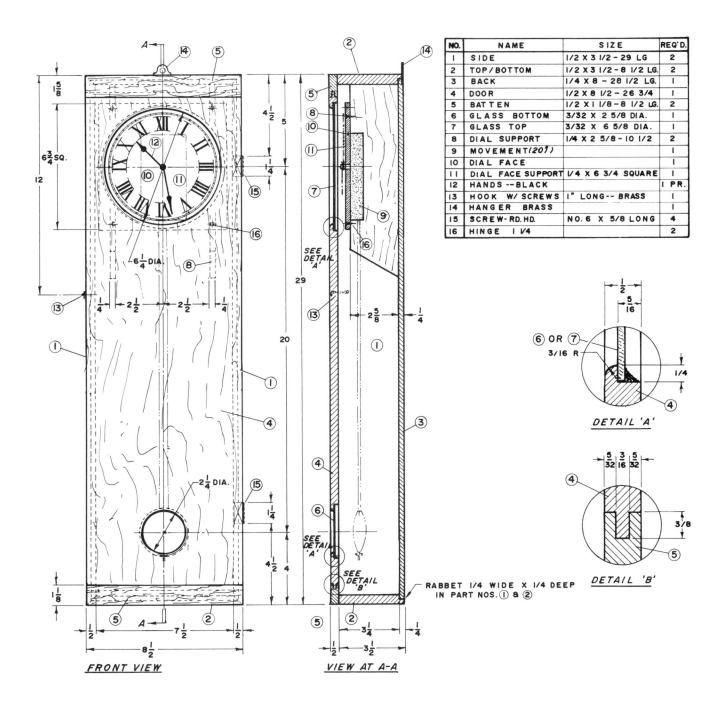

NO.	NAME	SIZE	REQ'D.
1	SIDE	1/2 X 3 1/2 - 29 LG	2
2	TOP/BOTTOM	1/2 X 3 1/2 - 8 1/2 LG.	2
3	BACK	1/4 X 8 - 28 1/2 LG.	1
4	DOOR	1/2 X 8 1/2 - 26 3/4	1
5	BATTEN	1/2 X 1 1/8 - 8 1/2 LG.	2
6	GLASS BOTTOM	3/32 X 2 5/8 DIA.	1
7	GLASS TOP	3/32 X 6 5/8 DIA.	1
8	DIAL SUPPORT	1/4 X 2 5/8 - 10 1/2	2
9	MOVEMENT (20?)		1
10	DIAL FACE		1
11	DIAL FACE SUPPORT	1/4 X 6 3/4 SQUARE	1
12	HANDS -- BLACK		1 PR.
13	HOOK W/ SCREWS	1" LONG -- BRASS	1
14	HANGER BRASS		1
15	SCREW - RD. HD.	NO. 6 X 5/8 LONG	4
16	HINGE 1 1/4		2

FRONT VIEW

VIEW AT A-A

DETAIL 'A'

DETAIL 'B'

RABBET 1/4 WIDE X 1/4 DEEP IN PART NOS. ① & ②

Using a 3/16-inch radius router bit with a ball-bearing follower, "round" the front edge of the two round openings—see detail 'A.' Turn the door over, and, using a router with a rabbet bit and ball-bearing follower, cut a recess for the glass 5/16-inch deep, as shown in detail 'A.' Sand all over.

Notch the right side of the case for the hinges. Locate the hinges up and down 4 1/2 inches, as shown. Temporarily mount the door with the hinges. Check to see that the door fits and closes correctly; make adjustments as necessary. Temporarily locate and add the brass hanger on top and the door hook on the left side.

Cut to size and sand the dial face support and dial supports. Glue the dial supports in place, as shown, and then screw the dial face support in place.

Glue the dial face to the dial face support, taking care to position it properly in the upper opening.

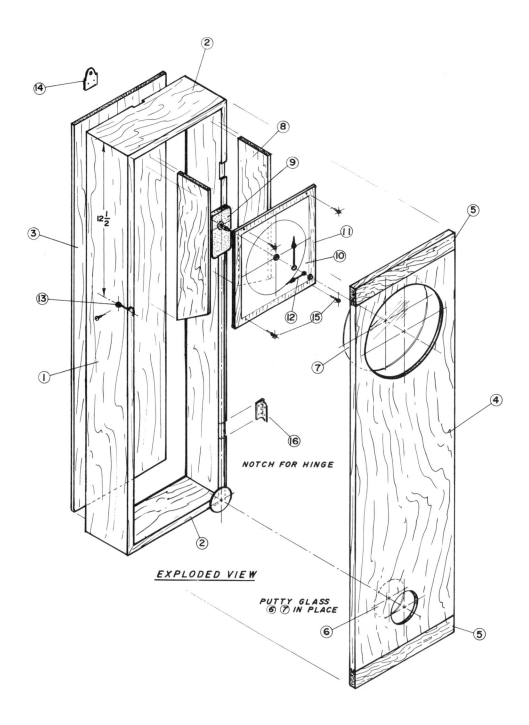

EXPLODED VIEW

NOTCH FOR HINGE

PUTTY GLASS
⑥ ⑦ IN PLACE

Finishing

Remove all of the hardware, and sand the case.

Because this is a copy of an old clock, I decided to give my clock some added authenticity by lightly distressing the case. Do any distressing before applying stain and top coats. Stain and apply two coats of a clear satin finish. Go over lightly with steel wool, and apply a coat of paste wax. Reattach all of the hardware; install the movement and hands. Add the glass—hold in place with black putty, as shown in detail 'A.' Finally, attach the pendulum, and your "antique" clock is ready to hang on the wall.

Although this clock is simply a box with a lid, it adds the elegance of simplicity—formal, yet stately—to any room it is hung in.

42 ♦ Tambour Shelf Clock

This is an exact copy of a clock I found in Wakefield, Rhode Island. Actually, I generally don't like tambour clocks, but I really liked this one. Tambour clocks became popular around 1910; they replaced the really ugly, Victorian "black" mantel clocks. The height of their popularity lasted through 1940 or so. Even today you can purchase a new, quartz-movement tambour-style clock.

I had an antique eight-day, gong strike, brass clock movement that I used on my version. If you would like to use an original movement, visit a local clock repair shop—they usually have all sorts of parts and mechanisms available. Bring the plans, and tell them it is a standard tambour clock. It will take a little extra "fitting," but well worth the effort. I find it particularly satisfying to put back in use a movement that is over fifty years old. The restored mechanism and authentic clock face will add a lot to your case.

Instructions

You will need two large pieces of wood for the two sides—each 3 13/16 inches by 4 3/8 inches and 13 inches long. If you don't have wood that size, you will have to glue up 3/4-inch stock to the needed size. Glue up the two pieces slightly larger than needed, and trim down to size after the glue sets. Study the exploded view, and be sure you fully understand how everything is made and goes together before starting.

Carefully lay out the full-size face on a 1/2-inch grid. Transfer the pattern to the wood, and cut it out. Using the face as part of the pattern, lay out the outer surface of the sides. Carefully lay out the inner surface of the sides. Be sure to maintain the 90 degree angle exactly as shown on the drawings. Carefully cut the two matching sides with a band saw. On the right side, locate and cut a shelf for the door latch, 5/16 of an inch in from the *back* edge. I used a 1 1/4-inch diameter Forstner bit and drilled in at an angle, trimming parallel to the back edge with a chisel.

Glue the two sides together at the top, and glue the face to the two sides. When the glue sets, sand all of the edges to form one smooth finish, up and over the entire length. I used a drill press with a three-inch sanding drum to sand the sides. Keep both sides exactly the same.

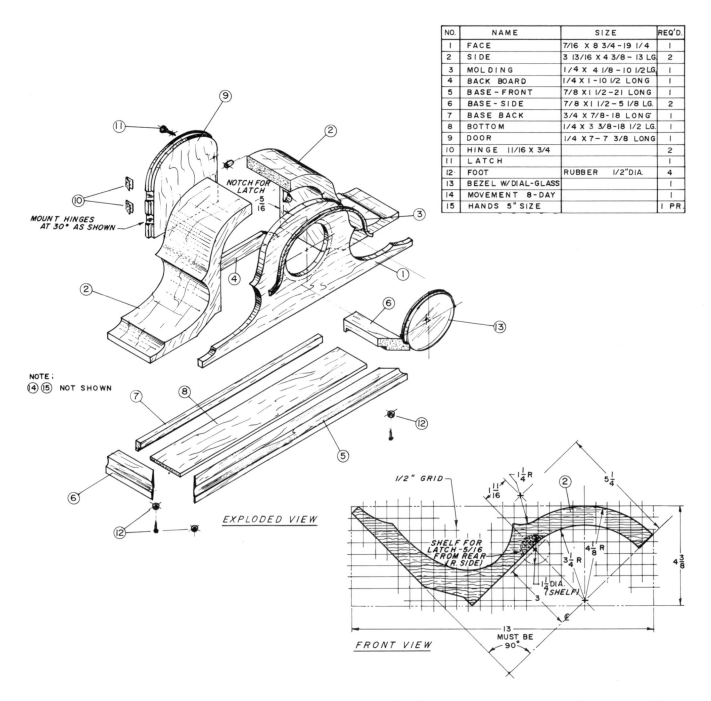

NO.	NAME	SIZE	REQ'D.
1	FACE	7/16 X 8 3/4 - 19 1/4	1
2	SIDE	3 13/16 X 4 3/8 - 13 LG.	2
3	MOLDING	1/4 X 4 1/8 - 10 1/2 LG.	1
4	BACK BOARD	1/4 X 1 - 10 1/2 LONG	1
5	BASE - FRONT	7/8 X 1 1/2 - 21 LONG	1
6	BASE - SIDE	7/8 X 1 1/2 - 5 1/8 LG.	2
7	BASE BACK	3/4 X 7/8 - 18 LONG	1
8	BOTTOM	1/4 X 3 3/8 - 18 1/2 LG.	1
9	DOOR	1/4 X 7 - 7 3/8 LONG	1
10	HINGE	11/16 X 3/4	2
11	LATCH		1
12	FOOT	RUBBER 1/2"DIA.	4
13	BEZEL W/DIAL-GLASS		1
14	MOVEMENT 8-DAY		1
15	HANDS 5" SIZE		1 PR.

NOTCH FOR LATCH 5/16

MOUNT HINGES AT 30° AS SHOWN

NOTE: (14) (15) NOT SHOWN

EXPLODED VIEW

1/2" GRID

SHELF FOR LATCH -5/16 FROM REAR (R. SIDE)

1 1/4 DIA. (SHELF)

FRONT VIEW

MUST BE 90°

Using the assembled face and sides as a pattern, lay out the top moulding directly on a piece of wood 1/4-inch thick, 4 1/8 inches wide, and 10 1/2 inches long. Important: cut only the *inner* edge at this time—this must be exactly three-eights of an inch *in* from the outer surface as determined by the face/side pattern. Using a router with a 3/16-inch radius cove bit and ball-bearing follower, rout the inner surface as shown. Now, cut the top surface; cut it about one-thirty-second of an inch larger. Glue the moulding to the face. When the glue sets, sand the top edge to match the top edge of the face and sides. Cut and fit the backboard to the back of the sides, and glue it in place. Sand the back edge.

Make up the pieces for the base front, sides, and back. Glue all of the base pieces together with the bottom in place to ensure 90 degree angles; refer to the exploded view. Sand all over. Turn over, and locate and drill holes for the feet.

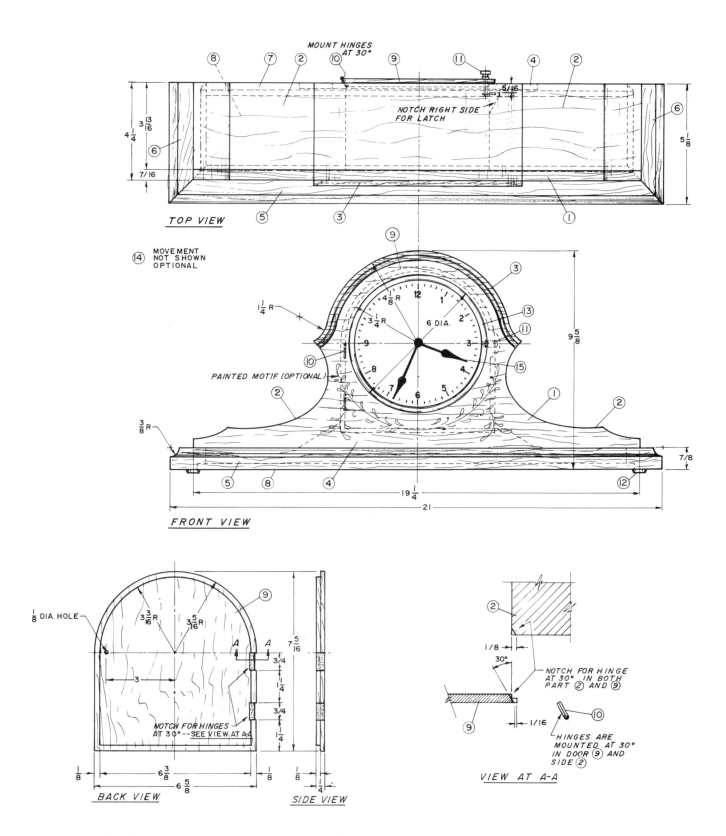

Lay out the door and cut it to size. You might want to use the case itself as a pattern for the inside edge of the door. Notch for the two hinges at about 30 degrees as shown in the top view; drill for the latch. Fit the door as shown in the exploded view and top view.

Glue the face and sides to the base assembly. Temporarily add the feet, door, and door latch. Check that everything fits and works correctly. Remove all of the hardware, and sand all over.

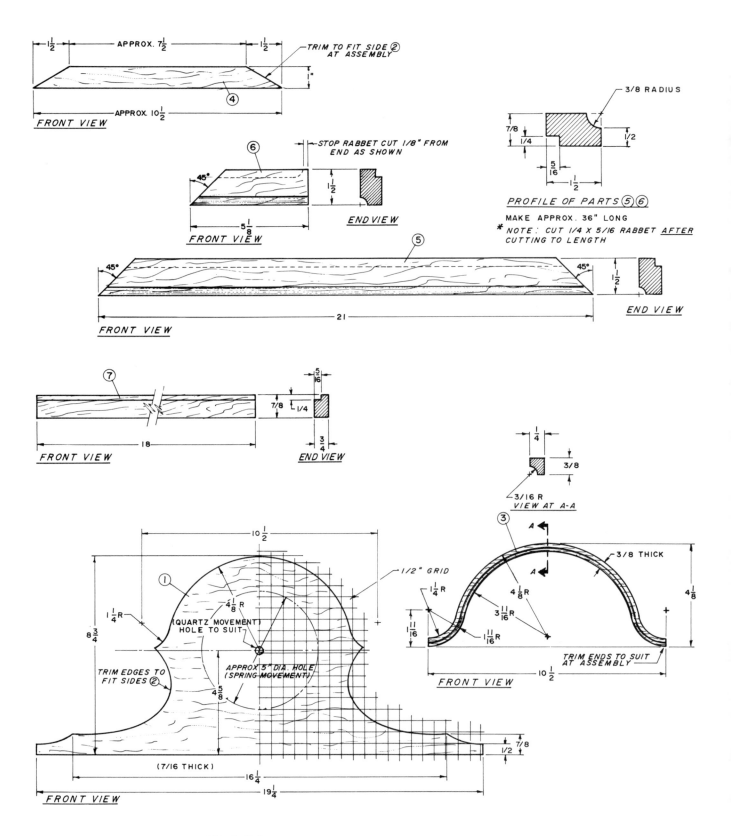

Finishing

Apply a stain of your choice and two or three coats of a clear, high-gloss finish.

Go over lightly with steel wool, and apply a coat of paste wax. Reattach all of the hardware; add the movement, dial, and hands. You now have a beautiful, faithful reproduction of an antique tambour clock—enjoy!

124

43 ♦ Shaker Wall Clock, circa 1840

A religious sect called the United Society of Believers in Christ's Second Appearing started in England around 1706. Because of their quivering and shaking during religious services, they became known as the Shakers. They believed that their furniture was originally designed in heaven and that the patterns were transmitted to them by angels; thus, their products had to be perfectly made, free from all blemishes. By 1840 there were about twenty colonies in the United States from Maine to Indiana. Shakers became well known for their fine furniture and products.

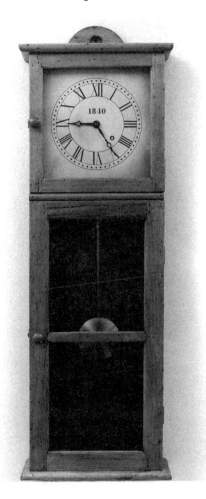

The Shaker elders were allowed to carry timepieces, but, for everyone else, such watches were considered an indulgence and unnecessary. Clocks, on the other hand, were indispensable and did not have the restrictions watches had.

There were actually only a very few Shaker clock makers—perhaps ten at the most. One of the most famous of these was Isaac Benjamin Youngs from Watervliet, New York. He was born July 2, 1793 and died at the age of 72 in 1865. He became the chief clock maker at the New Lebanon, New York, colony. Although Isaac built tall case clocks, his most well known clock is this relatively small wall clock. This clock was particularly interesting in that the backboard of the clock was also the backplate of the wooden-gear movement. Isaac Youngs was one of the few shaker craftsmen who wasn't afraid to experiment and to try innovative ideas.

This clock is a copy of a clock Isaac Youngs completed May 12, 1840 at the age of 47. The original is made of pine and has a light exterior stain and a dark-walnut stained interior.

Other similar wall clocks that Isaac made had solid wood panels in the lower door in place of the glass—even though this was thought to be very "frivolous." The original of this clock can be seen at the Shaker community in Hancock, Massachusetts—a visit that most woodworkers will really enjoy and appreciate.

Shakers never married nor bore children so their sect was only kept alive for a time by the acceptance of converts as new members. This led to the decimation of the sect, especially in combination with the changing economy after the Civil War; handcrafted products could no longer compete with lower cost, factory-made products.

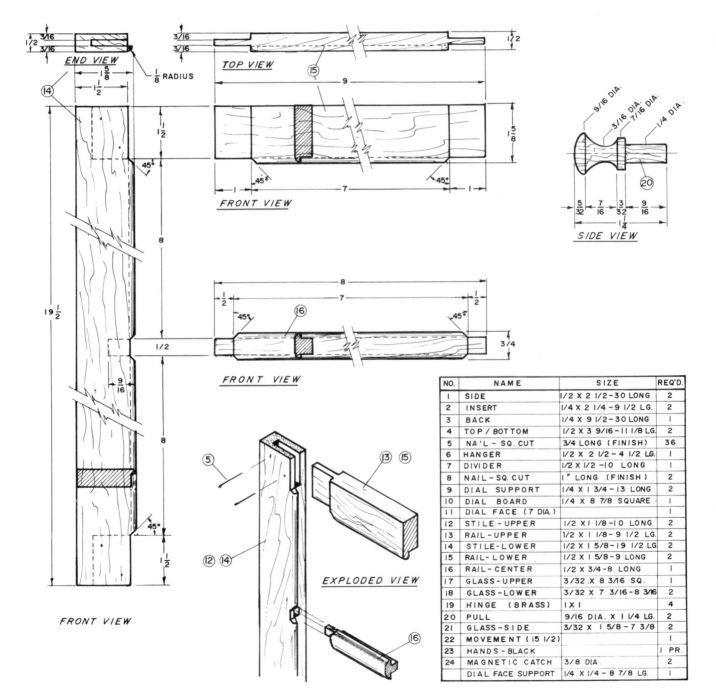

NO.	NAME	SIZE	REQ'D.
1	SIDE	1/2 X 2 1/2 – 30 LONG	2
2	INSERT	1/4 X 2 1/4 – 9 1/2 LG.	2
3	BACK	1/4 X 9 1/2 – 30 LONG	1
4	TOP / BOTTOM	1/2 X 3 9/16 – 11 1/8 LG.	2
5	NA'L – SQ. CUT	3/4 LONG (FINISH)	36
6	HANGER	1/2 X 2 1/2 – 4 1/2 LG.	1
7	DIVIDER	1/2 X 1/2 – 10 LONG	1
8	NAIL – SQ. CUT	1" LONG (FINISH)	2
9	DIAL SUPPORT	1/4 X 1 3/4 – 13 LONG	2
10	DIAL BOARD	1/4 X 8 7/8 SQUARE	1
11	DIAL FACE (7 DIA.)		
12	STILE – UPPER	1/2 X 1 1/8 – 10 LONG	2
13	RAIL – UPPER	1/2 X 1 1/8 – 9 1/2 LG.	2
14	STILE – LOWER	1/2 X 1 5/8 – 19 1/2 LG	2
15	RAIL – LOWER	1/2 X 1 5/8 – 9 LONG	2
16	RAIL – CENTER	1/2 X 3/4 – 8 LONG	1
17	GLASS – UPPER	3/32 X 8 3/16 SQ.	1
18	GLASS – LOWER	3/32 X 7 3/16 – 8 3/16	2
19	HINGE (BRASS)	1 X 1	4
20	PULL	9/16 DIA. X 1 1/4 LG.	2
21	GLASS – SIDE	3/32 X 1 5/8 – 7 3/8	2
22	MOVEMENT (15 1/2)		1
23	HANDS – BLACK		1 PR.
24	MAGNETIC CATCH	3/8 DIA.	2
	DIAL FACE SUPPORT	1/4 X 1/4 – 8 7/8 LG.	1

Instructions

Study all of the drawings very carefully; be sure you fully understand how the various parts are made and go together before starting. At the most basic level, you will see that this wall clock is not much more than a simple box with two lids—doors.

This project goes together quite quickly so you might want to order the parts in plenty of time so that you won't be held up waiting for the purchased parts.

Cut all of the parts to overall size according to the list of materials. Sand the surfaces with medium to fine grit sandpaper.

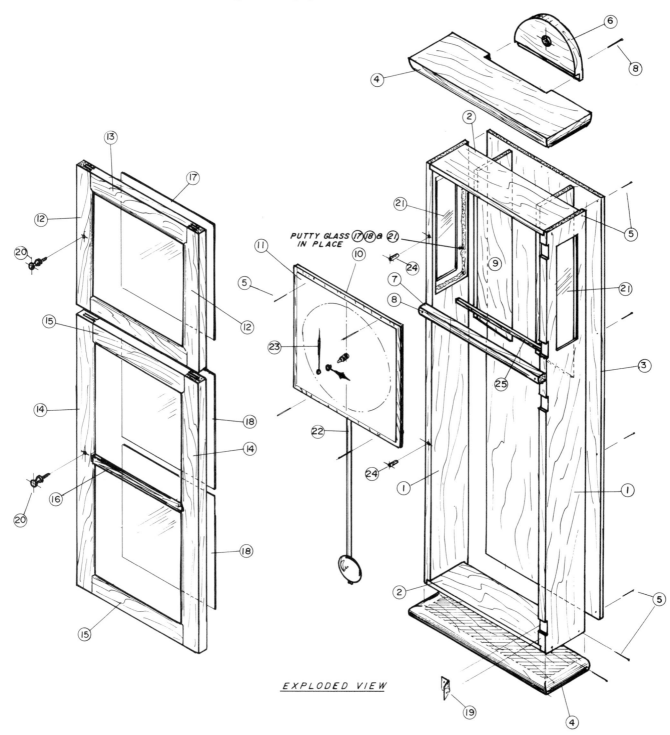

PUTTY GLASS 17 18 & 21 IN PLACE

EXPLODED VIEW

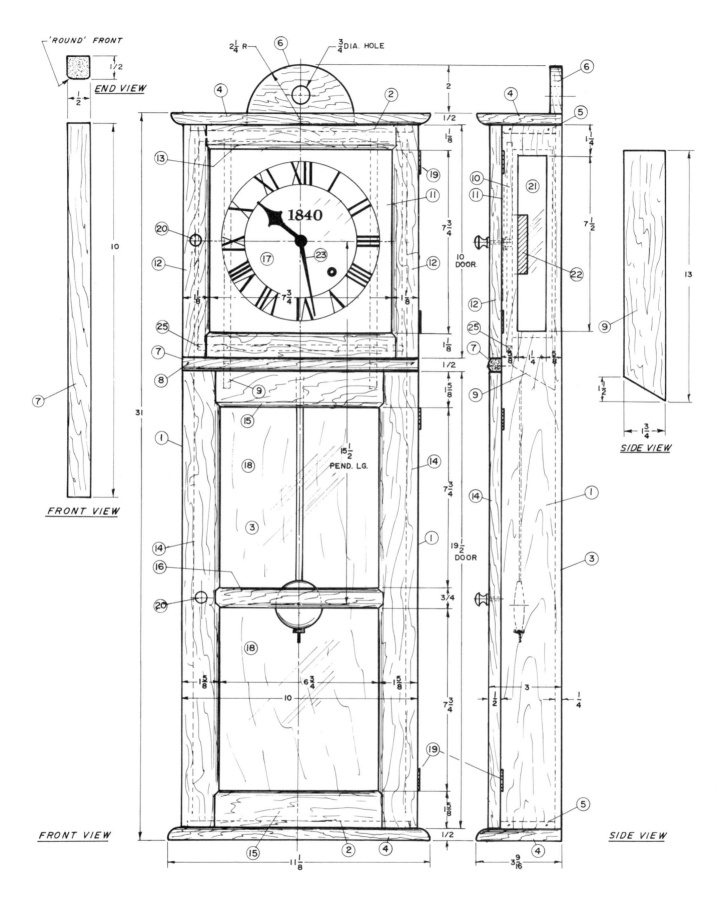

Note The original clock used a completely different dial face support. In the 1840 clock, the back of the movement was actually the back of the case. The dial face was attached to the movement.

The two dial supports used in this reproduction clock are the same design as those used in other, wooden weight-driven clocks of the same era.

Locate and cut out the 1 1/4-inch by 7 1/2-inch windows of the two sides, parts no. 1. Cut the 1/4-inch wide by 1/4-inch deep rabbet along the top, back, and bottom surfaces. Notch for the four hinges on the *right* side only. Resand all over, keeping all of the edges sharp.

Cut a 1/4-inch by 4 1/2-inch notch in the top only, part no. 4, as shown, and "round" the front and two sides.

Cut to shape the hanger, part no. 6, the divider, part no. 7, and the dial supports, part no. 9. Again, resand all parts keeping all edges sharp. Dry-fit the box assembly using the exploded view as a guide with part nos. 1 through 8—make any adjustments as necessary. When you're satisfied with the fit, apply very little glue and, for authenticity, use square cut nails. Set the divider, part no. 7, in place only temporarily—making adjustments later when doors are added as necessary.

If you want to see the movement, cut notches in the two dial supports, part no. 9, that line up with the windows in the sides, part no. 1. Check that the box is *square* before the glue sets—this is important. Cut the dial board, part no. 10, to size, and sand all over.

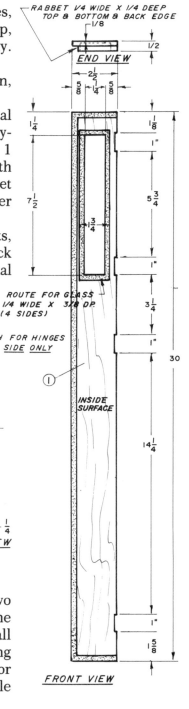

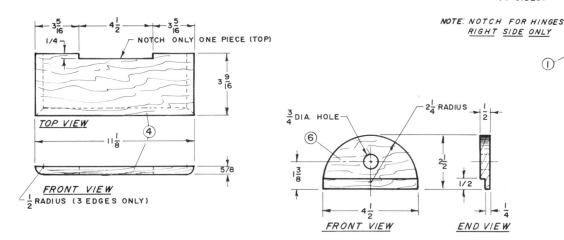

The only part of this project that is a little difficult is making the two doors; so take your time and measure as accurately as possible. Plane the material for the doors to 1/2-inch thickness. Cut the 1/8-inch radius on all door parts, part nos. 12 through 16. Notch for the glass as shown, making a 3/16-inch wide and 5/16-inch deep rabbet. Very carefully cut the door parts to size as indicated in the drawings. Work as accurately as possible so that you have a good-fitting door.

Dry-fit the door parts—also check that they fit with the case correctly. Make any adjustments as necessary. Glue the doors together; for extra strength and for an old "authentic" look, add the square cut nails, as shown.

After the glue sets, fill in any loose joints, and touch up as necessary. Sand all over, keeping all edges sharp. Do not try to hide the nails—they were not hidden on the original clocks. Turn the door pulls, part no. 20 and add them to the doors. Locate and drill for the two round magnetic catches, part no. 24. Make a final fit of the doors, and temporarily add the hinges. Check again that everything fits correctly. Remove the hinges and doors; sand the doors and case using very fine grit sandpaper.

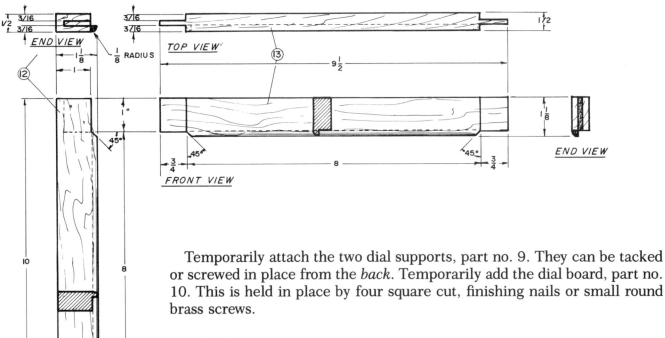

Temporarily attach the two dial supports, part no. 9. They can be tacked or screwed in place from the *back*. Temporarily add the dial board, part no. 10. This is held in place by four square cut, finishing nails or small round brass screws.

Finishing

Clean all surfaces with a tack rag, and apply a coat of pine stain to the outside of the case and to inside and outside of the two doors.

Add glass to the top door, and add two pieces of glass to the bottom door. Use a dark grey putty—if you can find it—for all of the glass.

Reattach the dial supports. Glue the dial face to the dial board, taking care that it is *centered* inside the *top door*—this is important! Drill a hole in the dial board for the shaft of the movement. Apply two coats of clear shellac; use steel wool between coats with no. 0000 wool. Apply a coat of paste wax to all exterior surfaces.

Reattach the two doors. Add a battery to the movement, and attach the movement to the dial face with a washer and nut. Screw or nail the dial board, with the movement and hands attached, to the dial supports.

Add the pendulum; hang the clock on a peg, and give the pendulum a push. Time is on your side—with luck *your* clock will last for 150 years, too.

COUNTRY PROJECTS

44 ◆ Lollypop-Style Wall Box

This is a copy of a simple wall box I found in northern Massachusetts. It probably was used for candles. The original was made of pine and painted a dark brick red color. This project is very easy to make as it has simple butt joints throughout.

Instructions

Cut all of the pieces to size, and sand all surfaces. Make a full-size pattern of the back, and transfer the pattern to the wood. Locate and drill the 3/4-inch diameter hole. Cut the back out and sand all the edges. Assemble with glue and nails. The nails on the original wall box were showing; so don't attempt to hide them unless they bother you. Round all of the edges slightly.

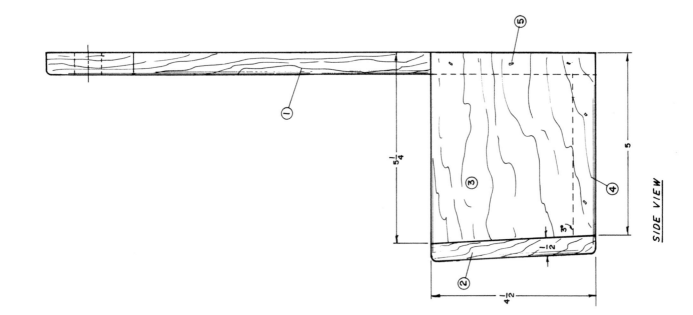

SIDE VIEW

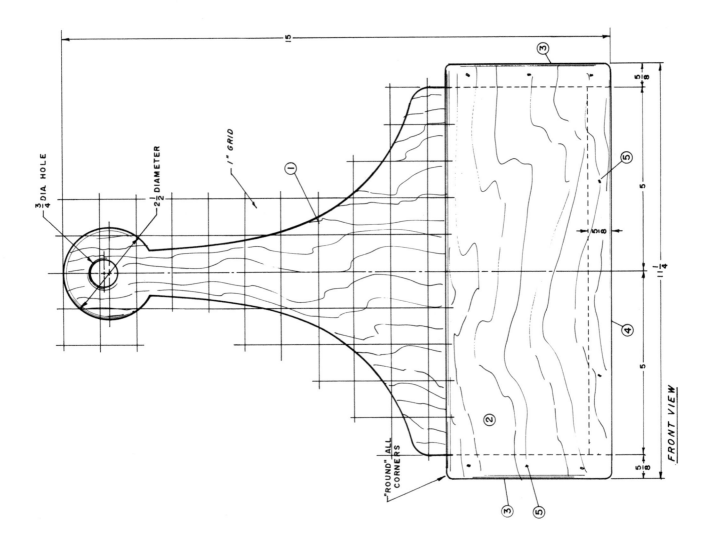

$\frac{3}{4}$ DIA HOLE

$2\frac{1}{2}$ DIAMETER

1" GRID

"ROUND" ALL CORNERS

FRONT VIEW

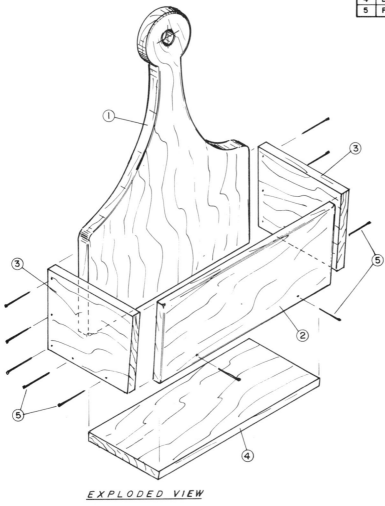

NO.	NAME	SIZE	REQ'D.
1	BACK	5/8 X 10 – 15 LONG	1
2	FRONT	1/2 X 4 1/2 – 11 1/4 LG.	1
3	END	5/8 X 4 1/2 – 5 1/4 LG.	2
4	BOTTOM	5/8 X 4 7/16 – 10 LG.	1
5	FINISH NAIL	4d	18

EXPLODED VIEW

Finishing

Paint or stain as you desire. This project is perfectly suited to distressing slightly and sanding the edges to give that old "worn" look. Hang it on the wall—add candles and you will be ready for that next power failure.

45 ◆ Pipe Box

This pipe box makes a great place to store candles; matches can be stored in the drawer. Or it could be an outgoing mail box instead, with stamps in the drawer. You may have some other ideas, such as an attractive place for displaying dried flowers.

Instructions

Make a 1/2-inch grid on a sheet of heavy paper, and lay out the top portions of the back, front, and sides. Cut all wood to overall size, and then transfer the patterns to the back, front, and side pieces. Cut all of these pieces to exact size following the patterns. Dry-fit all of the parts; trim as necessary. Glue and nail all pieces together, making sure that all parts are *square*.

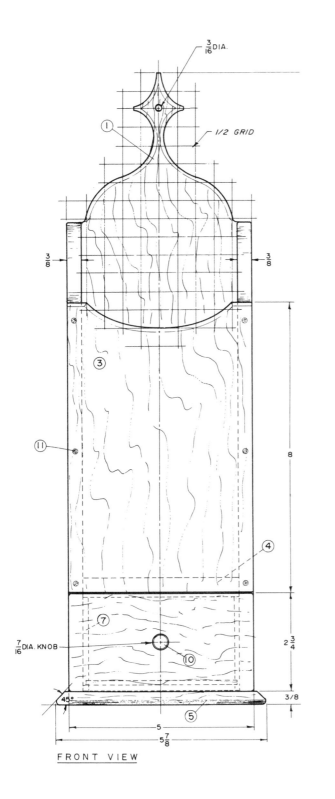

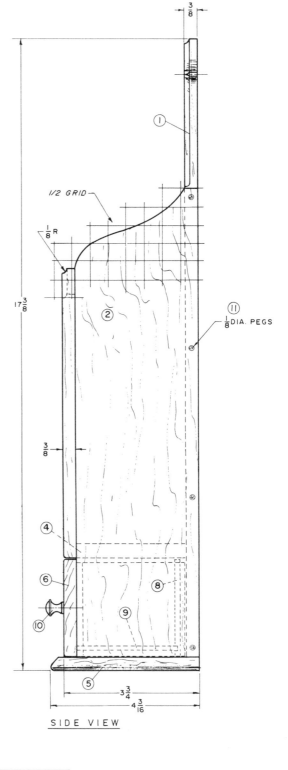

FRONT VIEW

SIDE VIEW

NO	NAME	SIZE	REQ'D.
I	BACK BOARD	3/8 X 4 1/4 - 17 LG.	I
2	SIDE	3/8 X 3 3/8 - 12 7/8	2
3	FRONT	3/8 X 5 - 8 LONG	I
4	DIVIDER	3/8 X 3 - 4 1/4 LONG	I
5	BOTTOM	3/8 X 4 3/16 - 5 7/8	I
6	DRAWER FRONT	1/2 X 2 3/4 - 5 LG.	I
7	" SIDE	3/16 X 2 3/4 - 3 LG.	2
8	" BACK	3/16 X 2 3/4 - 4 1/8	I
9	" BOTTOM	1/8 X 2 3/4 - 4 1/8	I
10	PULL (WOOD)	7/16 DIA.	I
11	PEG	1/8 DIA. X 3/4 LG.	18

135

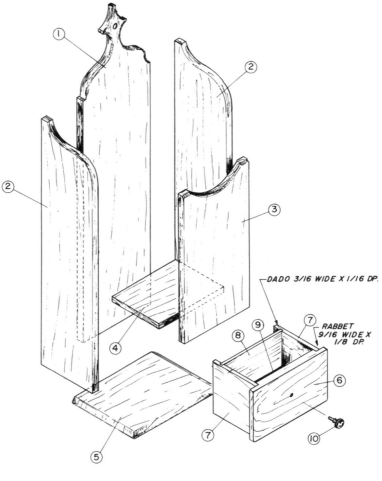

EXPLODED VIEW

The drawer is a simple design, easy to make. Make up the pieces, as shown in the exploded view, to fit the opening of the pipe box. Make the drawer front slightly larger so that it can be trimmed to fit the pipe box exactly. The drawer pull can be turned on a lathe to match the drawing or a 7/16-inch diameter commercially made one can be used.

Finishing

Your pipe box should be stained as you desire. If you'd rather not use it for candles or mail, someone could take up pipe smoking! On second thought, why not take up drying flowers; it's healthier!

46 ◆ Milking Stool

This is an exact copy of an antique milking stool that I found in Antrim, New Hampshire. This sturdy little stool was so unusual, I just *had* to draw up the plans. The original was made of maple and had worn-off paint from many years of hard use. This stool would have been used in the days when farmers actually milked their cows by hand.

Instructions

Because of the delicate, long legs, this project must be made of a hardwood for sufficient strength. Cut all of the pieces to size. Carefully lay out the oval for the top using the 5-inch radius and 10-inch radius, as shown in the top view. Cut out the top and sand around the edges. Using a 1/4-inch cove-cutter with a ball-bearing follower, cut the cove around the *top* surface of the stool top.

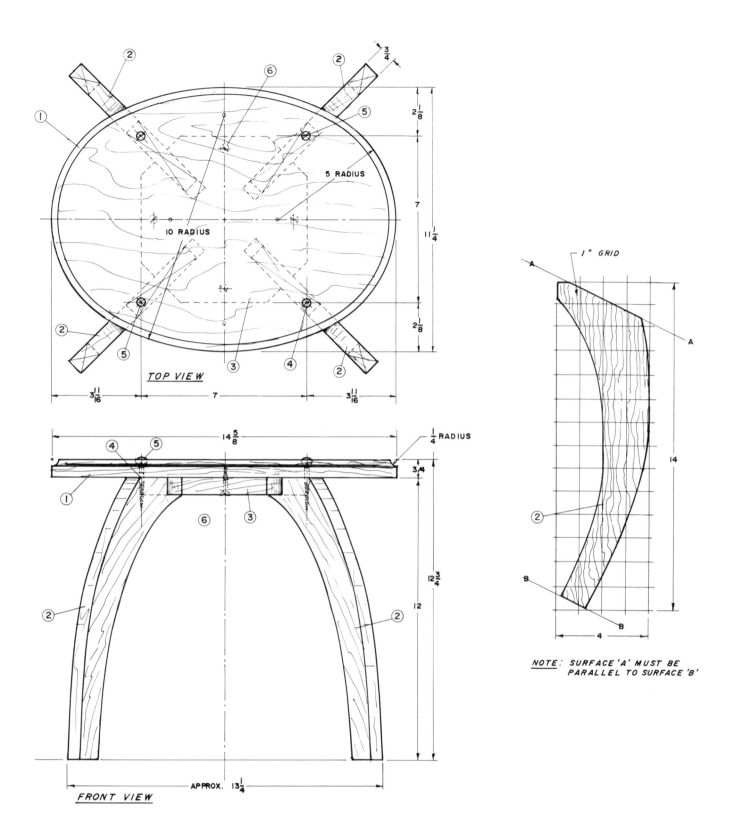

TOP VIEW

FRONT VIEW

NOTE: SURFACE 'A' MUST BE PARALLEL TO SURFACE 'B'

Lay out the legs using a one-inch grid, as shown. I taped all four legs together when I cut and sanded them so that all four would be exactly the same size and shape. Be sure to make the top of the legs *exactly* as shown. The unique angle, at the top of each leg, is designed to fit and lock into the support for added strength.

NO.	NAME	SIZE	REQ'D.
1	TOP	3/4 X 11 1/4 – 14 5/8	1
2	LEG	3/4 X 4 – 14 LONG	4
3	SUPPORT	3/4 X 7 SQUARE	1
4	SCREW–FLAT HEAD	NO. 8 2 1/2 LONG	4
5	PLUG	TO SUIT	4
6	SCREW–FLAT HEAD	NO. 8 1 1/4 LONG	4

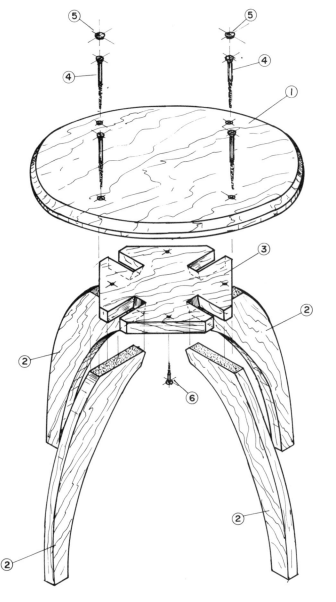

EXPLODED VIEW

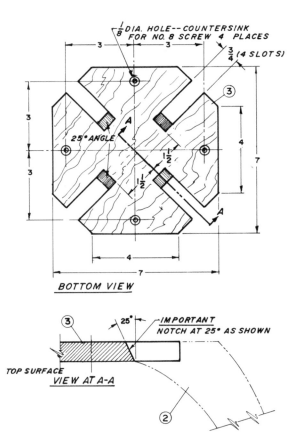

BOTTOM VIEW

VIEW AT A-A

The support also must be laid out and cut exactly as shown—especially the 25 degree notch designed to lock in and give the legs strength and support. Locate, drill, and countersink for all screws in all of the pieces, as shown. Dry-fit all of the pieces; check that the legs fit up and into the support notches. Make any adjustments as necessary. Glue and screw all of the pieces together.

Finishing

The stool should be primed and painted as you desire. This project—just like the footstool, project eleven—is perfect for rosemaling or tole painting. You might want to sand the edges slightly to reflect the "wear" of all those "years of milking."

47 ◆ Fish-Tail-Design Wall Box

This interesting wall box has the old familar fish tail design. It probably was made at or near an early American fishing community. I took the liberty to use an already split piece of wood for the front to give it that "real old" look. This also helped get rid of some otherwise unusable wood.

Instructions

On a one-inch grid, carefully lay out the fish tail on the back piece. Notch for the two side pieces. Cut the top and bottom edges of the front at 5 degrees, as shown. Cut the *front* edge of the bottom also at 5 degrees while the saw is still set at 5 degrees. Lay out the two matching sides—4 1/8 inches

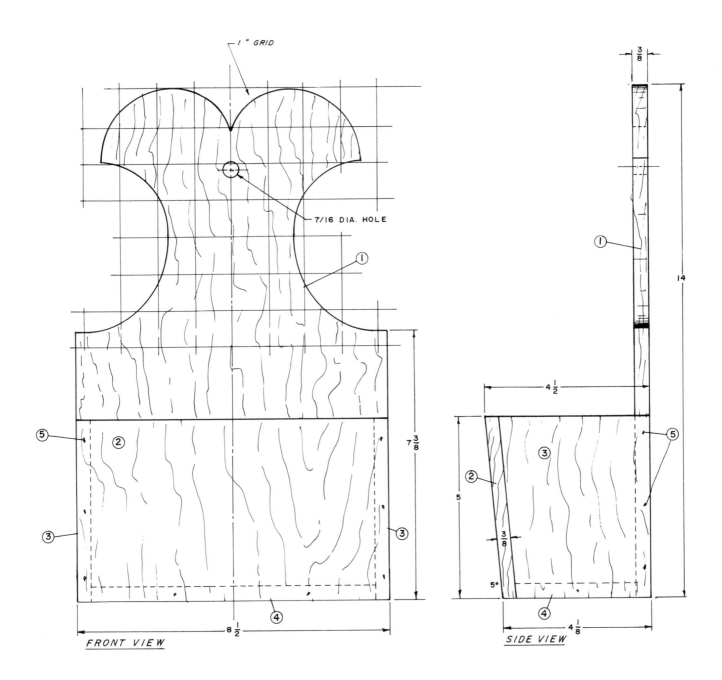

― 1" GRID

7/16 DIA. HOLE

FRONT VIEW

8 1/2

7 3/8

SIDE VIEW

3/8

14

4 1/2

5

3/8

5°

4 1/8

NO.	NAME	SIZE	REQ'D.
1	BACK	3/8 X 8 1/2 - 14 LG.	1
2	FRONT	3/8 X 8 1/2 - 5 1/8	1
3	SIDE	3/8 X 4 1/8 - 5 LONG	2
4	BOTTOM	3/8 X 3 3/4 - 7 3/4	1
5	SQ. CUT FIN. NAIL	1" LONG	16

at the top, 3 3/4 inches at the bottom—to make an approximate 5 degree cut, as shown in the side view. Sand all of the pieces. Dry-fit the box; if the fit is all right, glue and nail the box together, keeping everything square. Sand all of the edges slightly.

EXPLODED VIEW

Finishing

Distress and paint as you desire. I painted my copy with two coats of paint, and then I sanded through the top coat here and there where I thought it would have worn under normal use through the years.

48 ♦ Child's Small Chest of Drawers

The original chest of drawers from which this project is drawn was made expressly for Master Joseph Warren of Boston, Massachusetts in 1745. He used the chest of drawers as his toy chest. (Incidentally, Joseph later became a doctor and eventually lost his life at the battle of Bunker Hill in 1775 at the age of 34.) Today, this small chest of drawers can be used as a jewelry box or even as a child's toy chest—just as the original chest.

Instructions

Cut all of the pieces to exact size and sand all edges. Carefully locate and cut the three 1/4-inch wide, 1/8-inch deep dadoes in each side. Cut the 1/4-inch wide, 1/8-inch deep rabbet on the back edge of the sides. Important: be sure to make a right-hand and left-hand *pair* of sides. Using a 1/4-inch radius cove-cutter, cut the cove around the two ends and *front* of the top. Glue together the sides, dividers, and back. Sand all over.

Using a 1/4-inch grid, lay out the leg detail, as shown in the side view. Using a router bit with an ogee cutter, cut the top edge of the front and side skirt. Temporarily fit the front and two side skirts to the case using a 45 degree mitre cut at the corners, as shown. Remove the skirts and transfer the leg pattern to each skirt. Cut them out, and permanently reattach the skirts. Add the top. Make up the drawers to fit the openings. The drawers are the flush type, but they should fit with a little room for any expansion.

The six pulls can be turned to the 3/8-inch diameter. I made mine up from 3/8-inch diameter dowel. The original chest of drawer pulls were pinned in place, as shown; I did not use the pins, but simply glued the pulls in place instead.

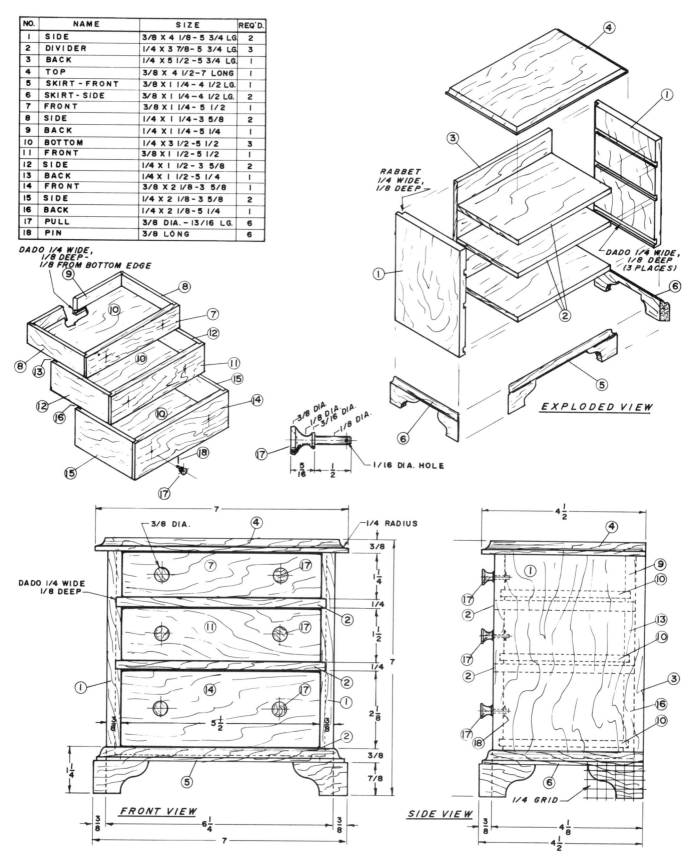

NO.	NAME	SIZE	REQ'D.
1	SIDE	3/8 X 4 1/8 - 5 3/4 LG.	2
2	DIVIDER	1/4 X 3 7/8 - 5 3/4 LG.	3
3	BACK	1/4 X 5 1/2 - 5 3/4 LG.	1
4	TOP	3/8 X 4 1/2 - 7 LONG	1
5	SKIRT - FRONT	3/8 X 1 1/4 - 4 1/2 LG.	1
6	SKIRT - SIDE	3/8 X 1 1/4 - 4 1/2 LG.	2
7	FRONT	3/8 X 1 1/4 - 5 1/2	1
8	SIDE	1/4 X 1 1/4 - 3 5/8	2
9	BACK	1/4 X 1 1/4 - 5 1/4	1
10	BOTTOM	1/4 X 3 1/2 - 5 1/2	3
11	FRONT	3/8 X 1 1/2 - 5 1/2	1
12	SIDE	1/4 X 1 1/2 - 3 5/8	2
13	BACK	1/4 X 1 1/2 - 5 1/4	1
14	FRONT	3/8 X 2 1/8 - 3 5/8	1
15	SIDE	1/4 X 2 1/8 - 3 5/8	2
16	BACK	1/4 X 2 1/8 - 5 1/4	1
17	PULL	3/8 DIA. - 13/16 LG.	6
18	PIN	3/8 LONG	6

Finishing

Distress very lightly; resand all over. A stain should be used, followed by a coat of satin finish tung oil or Danish oil.

144

49◆Double Candle Box

Besides being good for storing all sorts of things within easy reach, this double candle box makes a great planter. It is an unusual piece, if somewhat large. The construction is very simple as all of the joints are butt joints. The design is based on an original piece that was produced in Pennsylvania. The assembled box can be stained or painted. It will add a lot to any Early American decor.

Instructions

Cut all of the wood to size. Carefully, on a 1/2-inch grid, lay out the back, side, and two front pieces. Transfer the patterns to the wood, and cut to size. Sand all of the edges. For the two matching sides, tack or tape the pieces together, before cutting them out. The design for the top and bottom front pieces should also match so you might want to cut and sand them while they are tacked or taped together as well. Cut the front of the top and bottom bases at 8 degrees. Dry-fit all pieces. Nail and glue the pieces together. Leave the square cut nails showing since the original piece also left them exposed.

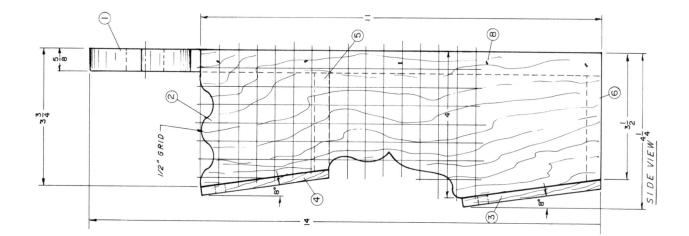

SIDE VIEW

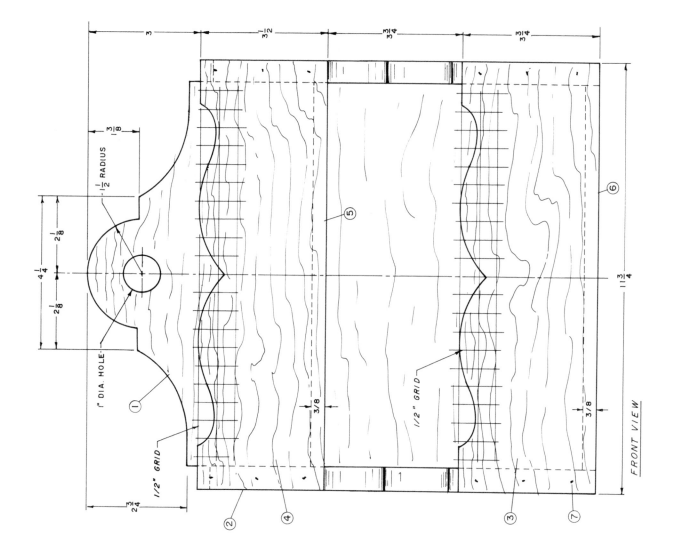

FRONT VIEW

1/2" GRID

1" DIA. HOLE

1½" RADIUS

NO.	NAME	SIZE	REQ'D.
1	BACK	5/8 X 14 – 10 1/2 LG.	1
2	SIDE	5/8 X 4 – 11 LONG	2
3	BOTTOM FRONT	1/4 X 3 3/4 – 11 3/4	1
4	TOP FRONT	1/4 X 3 1/2 – 11 3/4	1
5	TOP BASE	3/8 X 2 3/4 – 10 1/2	1
6	BOTTOM BASE	3/8 X 2 7/8 – 10 1/2	1
7	SQUARE CUT NAIL	3/4 LONG	12
8	SQUARE CUT NAIL	1 1/4 LONG	16

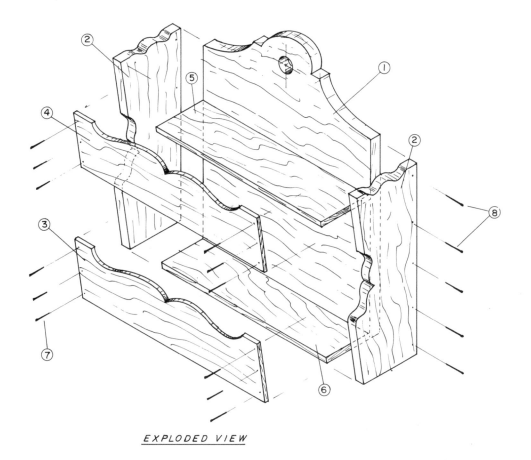

EXPLODED VIEW

Finishing

Finish the box as you desire; you can also decorate with stencils or tole painting. Now, you can enjoy using your candle box to grow some plants or to hold miscellaneous things—or even for *candles*; and with two box-fulls of candles you are ready for any sudden but seemingly endless power outage.

50 ◆ Small Queen Anne Mirror

Here is a small mirror that is perfect for a child's room or a small, formal entrance area. It will lend a "formal" look to any room. Mirrors such as this one—or the Chippendale mirror, project 51, that follows—are good projects to make for sale; they are easy to make, use hardly *any* material, and can sell for quite a lot, depending on the wood. Because so little wood is used, an expensive wood such as curly maple is a good choice, especially for resale purposes. The only extra cost is a special router bit; but if you make several, the bit is well worth the investment and can be used for many other projects later.

Instructions

Cut all of the pieces to size. Make up the moulding material for the rail and stile as one *long* piece of wood—3/4 inch by 7/8 of an inch and about 48 inches long—as shown in the profile view. Cut to size later using a good mitre box, as noted on the drawing.

Make a simple frame, 9 3/4 inches by 11 inches. Check that it is *square.* After the glue sets, cut for the 1/8-inch thick splines. Set the 45 degree cut three-sixteenths of an inch from the back edge, as shown in the side view. Add the splines, and sand all edges.

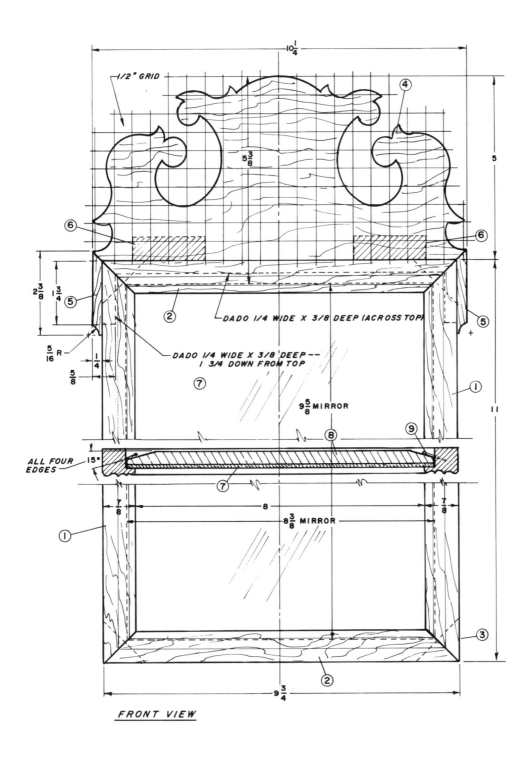

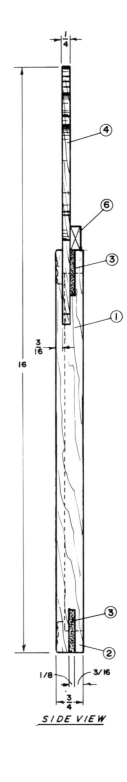

FRONT VIEW

SIDE VIEW

Using a router, carefully make a 1/4-inch wide notch for the top and side scrolls. Make this 1/4-inch wide groove in about three-sixteenths of an inch from the front surfaces, across the top edge, and down from the top on each side 1 3/4 inches, as shown in the front view. Resand all the outer edges.

On a 1/2-inch grid, lay out the top and side scroll patterns. Important: check to see that your 45 degree angle at the *ends* of the top scroll match the actual frame *you* made, not just the pattern as given. The plans call for a 9 3/4-inch wide frame, but yours might vary slightly; mine did. Adjust your scroll patterns as necessary. Transfer your patterns to the wood and cut them out. Attach the scroll pieces, and add the two braces to the back; sand all over.

149

NO.	NAME	SIZE	REQ'D.
1	STILE	3/4 X 7/8-11 LONG	2
2	RAIL	3/4 X 7/8-9 3/4 LG.	2
3	SPLINE	1/8 X 3/4-2 LONG	4
4	TOP SCROLL	1/4 X 5 3/8-10 1/4	1
5	SIDE SCROLL	1/4 X 5/8-2 3/8 LG.	2
6	BRACE	1/4 X 5/8-2 LONG	2
7	MIRROR	3/32 X 8 3/8 X 9 5/8	1
8	BACKBOARD	5/16 X 8 7/16-9 11/16	1
9	NAIL- SQUARE CUT	5/8 LONG	8

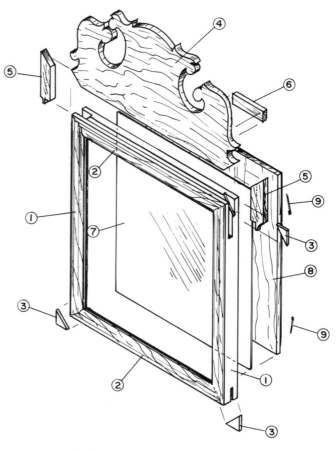

EXPLODED VIEW

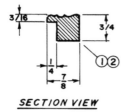

SECTION VIEW

Finishing

Apply two or three top coats of a satin finish. Add a coat of paste wax. Turn the mirror over and measure the *inside* size of the rabbet cut. Have a piece of mirror cut to size slightly smaller. Cut the backboard the same size as the mirror glass. Cut the outer edges of the backboard at 15 degrees, as shown. Secure the mirror and backboard with six or eight square cut, finishing nails, as shown. Add two eyescrews and picture frame wire, and you can go ahead and hang your mirror.

51 ♦ Chippendale Mirror

Not long ago my oldest daughter, Julie, wanted a fancy mirror for her bedroom. I looked around for full-size Chippendale mirrors, and quickly I concluded that I could draw up plans and build one less expensively than I could acquire one at the going prices. I did some research and came up with this design; it is a copy of an early Chippendale mirror.

The Chippendale period, as we now designate it, was from 1750 to 1785. The name derives from Thomas Chippendale of London, England, whose book of 1754 titled *The Gentleman and Cabinet Maker's Directory* widely popularized the furniture style characterized by graceful outline and ornate or elaborate ornamentation. It was the most complete and comprehensive furniture manual that had ever been published. The book provided inspiration for craftsmen in the American colony as well as in many other countries throughout the world.

A mirror such as this one should be made of hardwood such as mahogany, cherry, walnut or maple—preferably curley maple.

Instructions

Study the drawings very carefully to be sure that you fully understand how each piece is made and how the mirror is put together.

The profile of the frame moulding sides, top, and bottom, part nos. 1 and 2, can be made using a combination of router or shaper bits, but an exact profile can be made using the bit noted on the drawing.

Cut all of the pieces to overall size according to the cutting list. Sand all surfaces—progressing to a fine grit of sandpaper—this will save you from having to do a lot of finish sanding later.

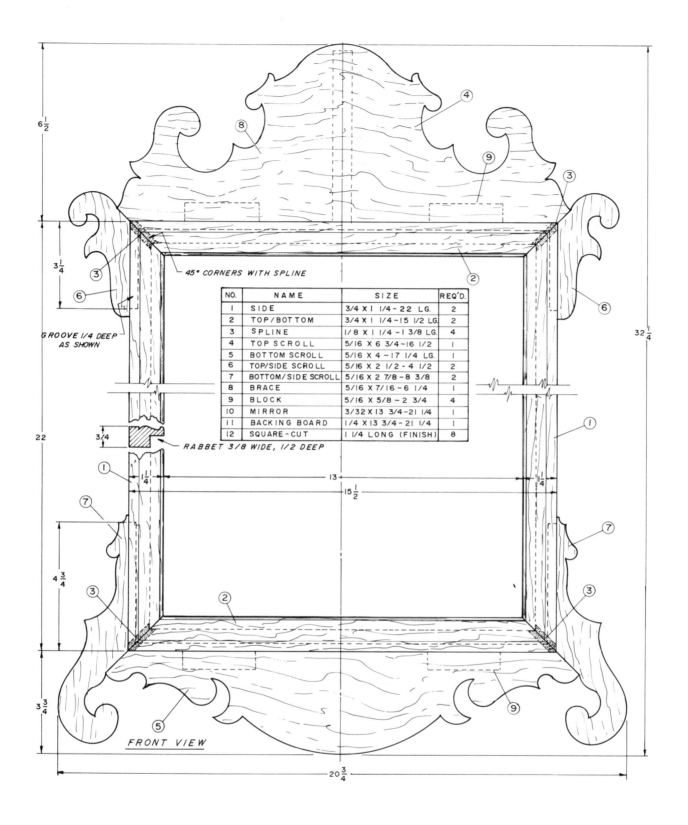

NO.	NAME	SIZE	REQ'D.
I	SIDE	3/4 X I 1/4 - 22 LG.	2
2	TOP/BOTTOM	3/4 X I 1/4 - 15 1/2 LG.	2
3	SPLINE	1/8 X I 1/4 - I 3/8 LG.	4
4	TOP SCROLL	5/16 X 6 3/4 - 16 1/2	I
5	BOTTOM SCROLL	5/16 X 4 - 17 1/4 LG.	I
6	TOP/SIDE SCROLL	5/16 X 2 1/2 - 4 1/2	2
7	BOTTOM/SIDE SCROLL	5/16 X 2 7/8 - 8 3/8	2
8	BRACE	5/16 X 7/16 - 6 1/4	I
9	BLOCK	5/16 X 5/8 - 2 3/4	4
10	MIRROR	3/32 X 13 3/4 - 21 1/4	I
I I	BACKING BOARD	1/4 X 13 3/4 - 21 1/4	I
12	SQUARE-CUT	I 1/4 LONG (FINISH)	8

45° CORNERS WITH SPLINE

GROOVE 1/4 DEEP
AS SHOWN

RABBET 3/8 WIDE, 1/2 DEEP

FRONT VIEW

Cut the profile shape of the face of the frame moulding, part nos. 1 and 2. It is a good idea to make a few extra pieces just in case you make an error in cutting later. Cut the rabbet, 3/8 inch by 1/2 inch, for the mirror, as shown. Cut the frame moulding pieces, making exact 45 degree cuts at the ends, and taking care to hold the exact lengths as dimensioned. Make the 1/8-inch wide by 1/4-inch deep grooves in the 45 degree cut for the splines, part no. 3. Important: note the direction of the grain in part no. 3.

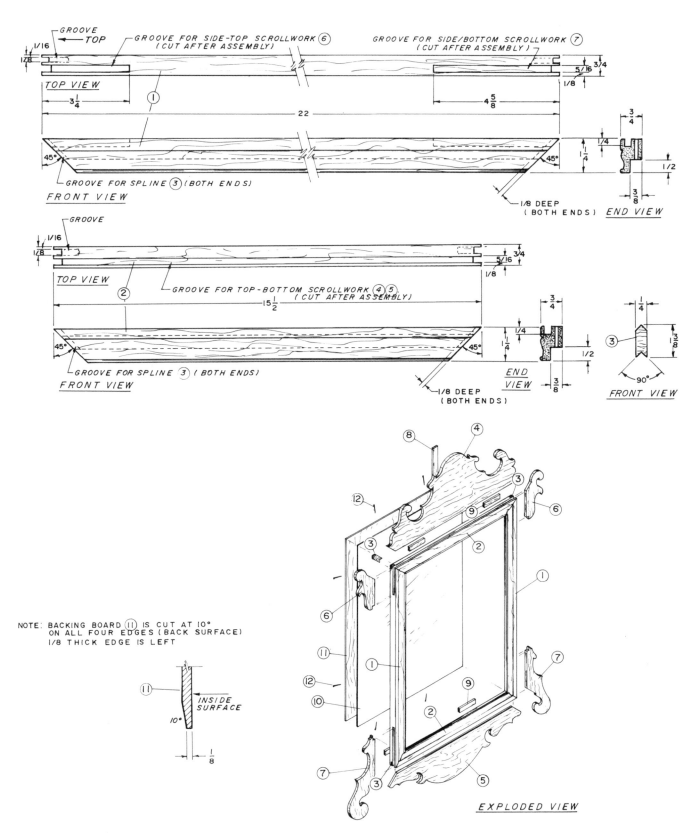

NOTE: BACKING BOARD ⑪ IS CUT AT 10°
ON ALL FOUR EDGES (BACK SURFACE)
1/8 THICK EDGE IS LEFT

EXPLODED VIEW

Glue the frame moulding pieces together, installing the splines as well. Be sure to keep all corners *exactly* 90 degrees. After the glue sets, cut the groove that will hold the scroll pieces along the top and bottom edges, as shown; cut the groove *down* from the top and *up* from the bottom as indicated on the plans. Transfer the full-size patterns of the scroll pieces, part nos. 4,5,6 and 7, to the wood.

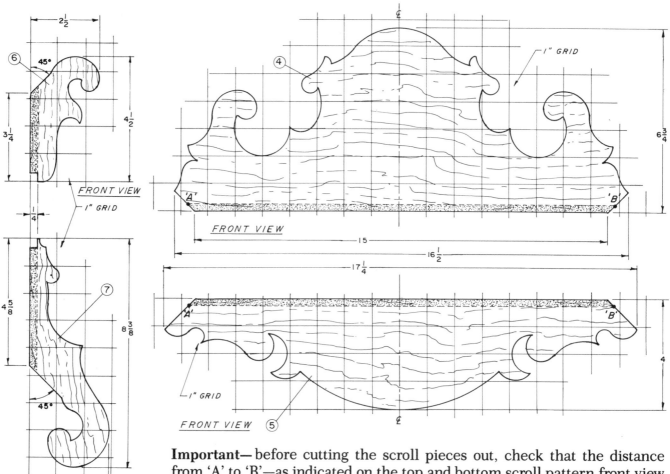

Important— before cutting the scroll pieces out, check that the distance from 'A' to 'B'—as indicated on the top and bottom scroll pattern front view layouts—is the exact same distance as the outside *width* of the frame *you* made. Adjust your pattern so that this distance *is* exactly the same as necessary; *This is important.* Carefully cut out the top and bottom scroll pieces, part nos. 4 and 5.

Tape together the two pieces of wood for the top side scrolls, part no. 6, and the two pieces of wood for the bottom side scrolls, part no. 7. Transfer each pattern and cut each set out as a pair. If necessary, sand them as a pair also.

All that is left to do now is to glue the scroll pieces and the brace to the frame subassembly. Attach the six scroll pieces; check for a good tight fit at the four, 45 degree mitre joints. After the glue sets, add the brace, and the four blocks. Resand all over, using very fine sandpaper.

Cut the backboard, part no. 11, to size. Taper all four edges at about 10 degrees or so—leave about an eighth of an inch on all four edges, as shown. Sand all over.

Finishing

Apply a light color stain as you desire, or leave it unstained. If you use a wood such as walnut, mahogany, or even cherry, you may not want to apply any stain. Apply four or five coats of a satin finish, such as tung oil. Lightly sand between coats using no. 0000 steel wool. Add a coat of paste wax, and your mirror frame is ready for adding the mirror.

Secure the mirror and the backboard with finishing nails.

Add picture frame eyehooks and wire between. Your Chippendale mirror is ready to hang.

52 ◆ Country Hutch with Two Drawers

As pewter and pottery plates began to replace wooden plates, the hutch became very popular. Many had two or three open shelves at the top to display the pewter and a closed cupboard underneath with one or two shelves. The early hutches came in all shapes and sizes, and typically they were built for a particular room or even for a specific place.

This hutch design is based on several designs I've collected of such typical early hutches. I took a few liberties to come up with a design that is both functional and pleasing in its lines.

Instructions

Study all of the drawings before starting. Note how the hutch is put together and how each part is made.

Cut all of the parts to overall size as given in the cutting list; take extra care to make 90 degree cuts. Carefully lay out and make the seven, 3/4-inch wide, 1/4-inch deep dado cuts and the 3/4-inch wide, 1/4-inch deep rabbet cuts (at the top on the two sides). Be sure all cuts on both sides match exactly.

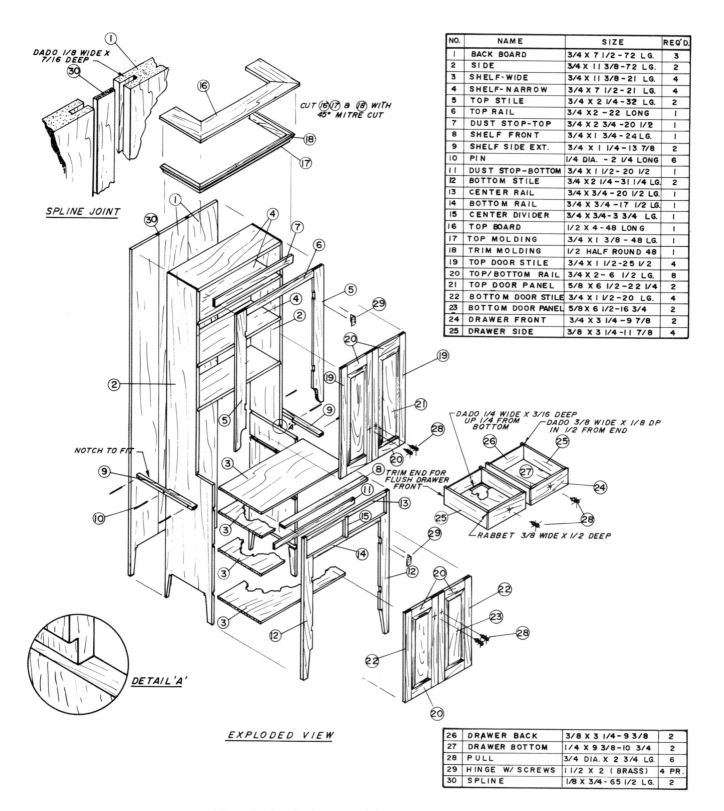

DADO 1/8 WIDE X 7/16 DEEP

SPLINE JOINT

CUT 16 17 & 18 WITH 45° MITRE CUT

NOTCH TO FIT

TRIM END FOR FLUSH DRAWER FRONT

DADO 1/4 WIDE X 3/16 DEEP UP 1/4 FROM BOTTOM

DADO 3/8 WIDE X 1/8 DP IN 1/2 FROM END

RABBET 3/8 WIDE X 1/2 DEEP

DETAIL 'A'

EXPLODED VIEW

NO.	NAME	SIZE	REQ'D.
1	BACK BOARD	3/4 X 7 1/2 - 72 LG.	3
2	SIDE	3/4 X 11 3/8 - 72 LG.	2
3	SHELF - WIDE	3/4 X 11 3/8 - 21 LG.	4
4	SHELF - NARROW	3/4 X 7 1/2 - 21 LG.	4
5	TOP STILE	3/4 X 2 1/4 - 32 LG.	2
6	TOP RAIL	3/4 X 2 - 22 LONG	1
7	DUST STOP - TOP	3/4 X 2 3/4 - 20 1/2	1
8	SHELF FRONT	3/4 X 1 3/4 - 24 LG.	1
9	SHELF SIDE EXT.	3/4 X 1 1/4 - 13 7/8	2
10	PIN	1/4 DIA. - 2 1/4 LONG	6
11	DUST STOP - BOTTOM	3/4 X 1 1/2 - 20 1/2	1
12	BOTTOM STILE	3/4 X 2 1/4 - 31 1/4 LG.	2
13	CENTER RAIL	3/4 X 3/4 - 20 1/2 LG.	1
14	BOTTOM RAIL	3/4 X 3/4 - 17 1/2 LG.	1
15	CENTER DIVIDER	3/4 X 3 3/4 - 3 3/4	1
16	TOP BOARD	1/2 X 4 - 48 LONG	1
17	TOP MOLDING	3/4 X 1 3/8 - 48 LG.	1
18	TRIM MOLDING	1/2 HALF ROUND 48	1
19	TOP DOOR STILE	3/4 X 1 1/2 - 25 1/2	4
20	TOP/BOTTOM RAIL	3/4 X 2 - 6 1/2 LG.	8
21	TOP DOOR PANEL	5/8 X 6 1/2 - 22 1/4	2
22	BOTTOM DOOR STILE	3/4 X 1 1/2 - 20 LG.	4
23	BOTTOM DOOR PANEL	5/8 X 6 1/2 - 16 3/4	2
24	DRAWER FRONT	3/4 X 3 1/4 - 9 7/8	2
25	DRAWER SIDE	3/8 X 3 1/4 - 11 7/8	4

NO.	NAME	SIZE	REQ'D.
26	DRAWER BACK	3/8 X 3 1/4 - 9 3/8	2
27	DRAWER BOTTOM	1/4 X 9 3/8 - 10 3/4	2
28	PULL	3/4 DIA. X 2 3/4 LG.	6
29	HINGE W/ SCREWS	1 1/2 X 2 (BRASS)	4 PR.
30	SPLINE	1/8 X 3/4 - 65 1/2 LG.	2

After all the dado and rabbet cuts have been made, locate and cut out the step in the sides. The step back should end up the same width as the three top shelves. It is dimensioned 7 1/2 inches wide, but if your top shelves measure 7 1/4 inches or 7 3/8 inches, make the step to match the width of the top shelves. Stop the step at the *bottom* of the fourth dado from the bottom—see detail 'A.' This is *important*; also be sure to make right-hand *and* left-hand sides with the dadoes and rabbet located on the *inside* surfaces.

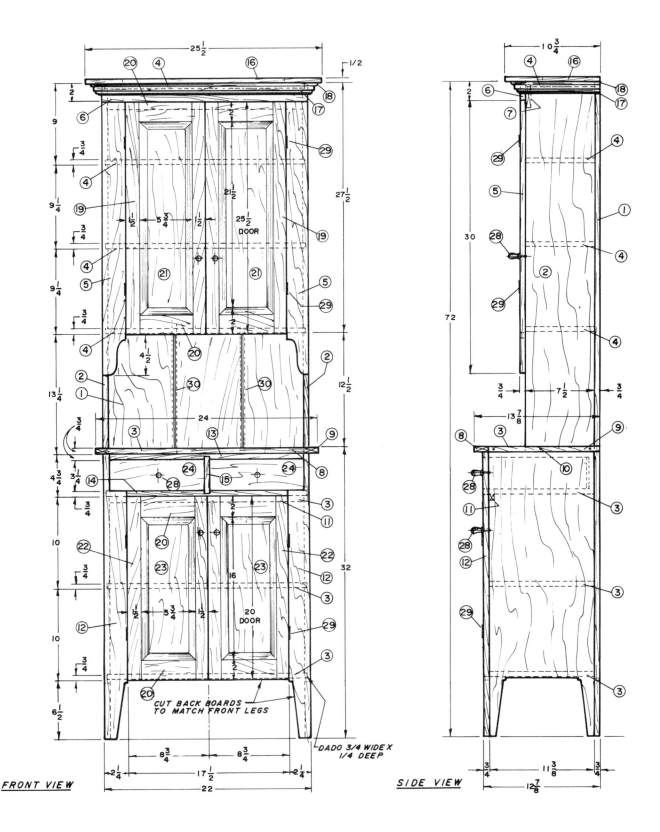

FRONT VIEW

SIDE VIEW

Glue and nail all the shelves and the top board in place, keeping the assembly exactly square. Check again before the glue sets that everything is exactly *square*. A "trick" that I use is to attach the backboards *before* the glue sets; this will ensure that everything is square. Note: the backboards have a 1/8-inch wide, 7/16-inch deep dado running along the inside edges so that a spline can be added to allow for any expansion—or contraction—preventing warping or cracking.

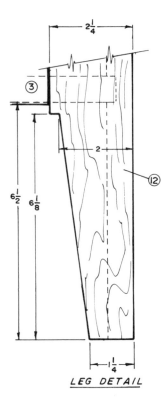

LEG DETAIL

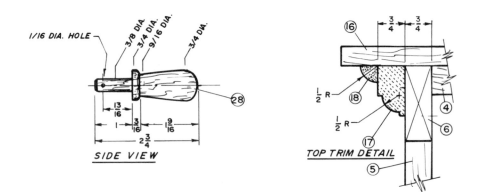

SIDE VIEW

TOP TRIM DETAIL

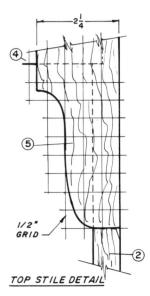

TOP STILE DETAIL

Carefully lay out and cut out the patterns for the legs on the sides and back—after the glue sets. Add the top and bottom dust-stop pieces. At this time sand the side and back using medium grit sandpaper. Be sure the edge of the outer backboards blend into the side pieces. Add the shelf front and the two shelf side extensions; the two side extensions will have to be notched to fit. Locate and add the three pins to help strengthen the side extensions.

Cut and fit the top stile and two rails; attach them to the case. Add the top board and top moulding using 45 degree mitre cuts, as shown in the exploded view. Fit the bottom stile with the bottom and center rails; notch as shown, and add the center divider.

Make up the two drawers to fit the two openings. Simple, flush drawers are shown but you can add overlapping drawers if you wish. The exploded view provides details for making simple, flush drawers.

Make up the two upper and lower doors, also as illustrated. If you have cutters for making raised panel doors, use them. If you do not have special cutters, use simple mortise-and-tenon joints for the doors—cut on a table saw. This project will look just fine with flat panel doors, if you prefer not making raised panel doors. Fit the doors to the openings. The door and drawer pulls can be purchased or made. If you do not have a lathe, you can make them using your table saw and a rasp. The pulls look older if they are *not* quite all exact; so don't be afraid to make them by hand. I made up those pictured with a table saw and rasp; my six are close but not exactly the same. Attach the pulls, as shown, using a 1/16-inch diameter wooden peg to hold them in place.

Finishing

Remove all of the hardware, and sand all over. Clean with a tack rag. This project can be stained and finished or painted. I distressed and painted the interior with a thinned coat of red paint to get a washed-out look. I then added two different colors—mustard and blue—and sanded through the blue in places to simulate "wear," exposing the first coat of mustard. For this piece, I then applied a coat of dark walnut stain and wiped it off immediately—ordinarily I would use thinned, black paint, but I was out of black paint at the time. Adding stain or black paint over the top coat brings out the distress marks and makes the hutch look much older. Reattach all of the hardware, and your country hutch is ready for years of service, already looking as if it has seen many generations sit down to countless meals.

Index

Metric Conversion

Inches to Millimetres and Centimetres

MM—millimetres   CM—centimetres

Inches	MM	CM	Inches	CM	Inches	CM
⅛	3	0.3	9	22.9	30	76.2
¼	6	0.6	10	25.4	31	78.7
⅜	10	1.0	11	27.9	32	81.3
½	13	1.3	12	30.5	33	83.8
⅝	16	1.6	13	33.0	34	86.4
¾	19	1.9	14	35.6	35	88.9
⅞	22	2.2	15	38.1	36	91.4
1	25	2.5	16	40.6	37	94.0
1¼	32	3.2	17	43.2	38	96.5
1½	38	3.8	18	45.7	39	99.1
1¾	44	4.4	19	48.3	40	101.6
2	51	5.1	20	50.8	41	104.1
2½	64	6.4	21	53.3	42	106.7
3	76	7.6	22	55.9	43	109.2
3½	89	8.9	23	58.4	44	111.8
4	102	10.2	24	61.0	45	114.3
4½	114	11.4	25	63.5	46	116.8
5	127	12.7	26	66.0	47	119.4
6	152	15.2	27	68.6	48	121.9
7	178	17.8	28	71.1	49	124.5
8	203	20.3	29	73.7	50	127.0